I vividly recall the initial v .... ter and Mr Don Philpott when they indicated their intention to augment Grenada's marketing efforts by producing a comprehensive, informative and colourful Guide Book about Grenada, Carriacou and Petit Martinique.

It is therefore with great pleasure that we at the Grenada Board of Tourism (GBT) welcome this timely addition to the tourism literature of our tri-island state. GBT is pleased to be associated with Mr Don Philpott and his team in the production of *Caribbean Sunseekers: Grenada*.

The tourism industry of this country has made great strides in recent years and is now poised for take off. As recently as 1983 Grenada welcomed 32,459 stayover visitors and 50,000 cruise ship passengers. Today, after 12 years of increases within both categories, and an increased room count from 500 to 1,500, visitor arrivals in 1994 reached 109,957 in the stayover category, and 200,808 in the cruise ship sector. With corresponding improvements in the country's infra-structure, the foundation has now been laid to build a truly balanced and sustainable tourism industry which will foster linkages with agriculture and manufacturing among others.

In synergy with these developments, the timely publication of *Caribbean Sunseekers: Grenada*, ideally complements Grenada's emphasis on quality tourism. The book traces in very sophisticated and picturesque measure, the colourful history of the nation from its pre colonial era to its present independent status. Its focus on the geological, environmental and natural vegetation of our country, coupled with its treatment of the cultural and historical attractions that make Grenada, Carriacou and Petit Martinique a truly unique destination, all contribute towards making it an inevitable choice for every visitor.

Additionally, its very informative general information section gives accurate guidance about accommodation options, restaurants, night life, watersports and other requisite activities of the discerning traveller.

It truly addresses the responses to questions that would logically surface amongst visitors and potential visitors alike, thus making it a perfect souvenir of our nation.

In endorsing this production, and in keeping with the usual warmth and hospitality of our 96,000 population, it gives me great pleasure to commend all those whose efforts contributed towards this product, while wishing you happy times as you turn these pages and proceed to put into practice the recommendations contained therein. Welcome to our beautiful isles of Spices.

Director of Tourism, Mr. G.R.E. Bullen

GRENADA

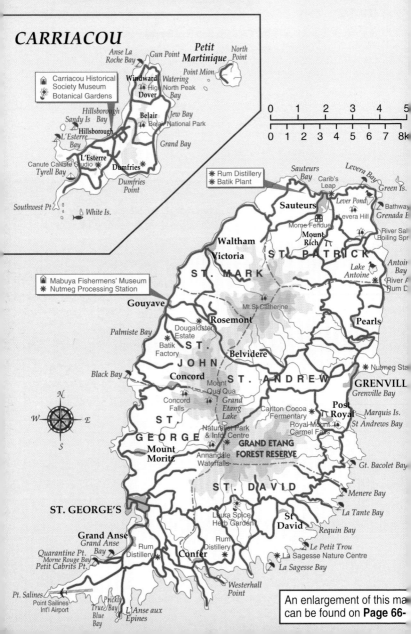

CARRIACOU

- Carriacou Historical Society Museum
- Botanical Gardens

Anse La Roche Bay
Gun Point
Petit Martinique
North Point
Point Mion
Watering
Windward
High North Peak Bay
Dover
Hillsborough Bay
Sandy Is
Hillsborough
L'Esterre Bay
Belair
Belair National Park
Jew Bay
Grand Bay
Canute Caliste Studio
Tyrell Bay
L'Esterre
Dumfries
Southwest Pt
White Is.
Dumfries Point

0 1 2 3 4 5
0 1 2 3 4 5 6 7 8k

- Rum Distillery
- Batik Plant

Sauteurs Bay
Carib's Leap
Levera Bay
Green Is.
Sauteurs
Lever Pond
Bathway
Levera Hill
Grenada B
River Sall
Boiling Spr
Morne Fendue
Mount Rich
Waltham
Victoria
ST. PATRICK
Lake Antoine
Antoin
Bay
River A
Rum D
ST. MARK
Mabuya Fishermens' Museum
Nutmeg Processing Station
Mt. St. Catherine
Gouyave
Rosemont
Pearls
Palmiste Bay
Dougaldston Estate
Batik Factory
ST. JOHN
Belvidere
Nutmeg Sta
Black Bay
Concord
ST. ANDREW
GRENVILL
Grenville Bay
Mount Qua Qua
Concord Falls
Grand Etang Lake
Carlton Cocoa Fermentary
Post Royal
Marquis Is.
St Andrews Bay
Naturalist Park & Info Centre
Royal Mount Carmel Falls
ST GEORGE
Mount Moritz
Annandale Waterfalls
GRAND ETANG FOREST RESERVE
Gt. Bacolet Bay
ST. DAVID
Menere Bay
ST. GEORGE'S
Laura Spice Herb Garden
St David
La Tante Bay
Requin Bay
Grand Anse
Grand Anse Bay
Rum Distillery
Confer
Le Petit Trou
La Sagesse Nature Centre
Quarantine Pt.
Morne Rouge Bay
Petit Cabrits Pt.
Rum Distillery
La Sagesse Bay
Pt. Salines
Point Sailines Int'l Airport
Prickly Bay
True Blue Bay
L'Anse aux Epines
Westerhall Point

An enlargement of this ma can be found on **Page 66-**

CARIBBEAN SUNSEEKERS
Grenada

Don Philpott

PASSPORT BOOKS
a division of *NTC Publishing Group*
Lincolnwood, Illinois USA

Published by Passport Books,
a division of NTC Publishing Group,
4255 West Touhy Avenue,
Lincolnwood (Chicago), Illinois
60646 – 1975 USA

ISBN 0 8442 4926 2

Library of Congress Catalog Card Number:
95-74812

Published by Passport Books in conjunction with
Moorland Publishing Company Ltd.

Color origination by: Reed Reprographics, Ipswich, England
Printed in Hong Kong by Wing King Tong Co Ltd

ACKNOWLEDGMENTS:
Edwin Frank and The Grenada Board of Tourism, True Blue Inn, Flamboyant Hotel, American Airways LIAT, and
Maeve Murphy.

PICTURE CREDITS:
Front cover: St. George's (main photo), Grand Anse Bay (inset). Back cover: St. George's harbour front. Title
page:Gouyave. All photographs are from the MPC Picture collection except: Chris Huxley (Caribbean Images) 23,
71, 106, 107, 126, 142/143, 150 Maeve Murphy 7, 47, 118/119, 123, 155 (bottom) Don Philpott 11

MPC Production Team:
Editor: Tonya Monk
Editorial assistant: Christine Haines
Designer: Dick Richardson
Cartographer: Mark Titterton

DISCLAIMER

While every care has been taken to ensure that the information in this book is as
accurate as possible at the time of publication, the publishers and author accept
no responsibility for any loss, injury or inconvenience sustained by anyone using
this book.

Your trip to the Caribbean should be a happy one, but certain activities such
as water sports should be approached with care and under proper supervision
when appropriate. It is also in your own interests to check locally about flora and
fauna that it is best to avoid.

Contents

KEY TO SYMBOLS USED IN TEXT MARGIN AND ON MAPS

🏃	Recommended walks	⌂	Church/Ecclesiastical site
🐟	Aquatic interest	🏛	Building of interest
🏰	Castle/Fortification	⊤	Archaeological site
✳	Other place of interest	🏛	Museum/Art Gallery
⛵	Beach	🏞	Beautiful view/Scenery, Natural phenomenon
⬤	Water sports	🐦	Birdlife
🌿	Garden	✈	Airport

KEY TO MAPS

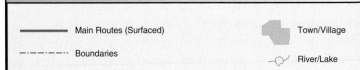

▬▬▬	Main Routes (Surfaced)	◼	Town/Village
▬ ▬ ▬	Boundaries	∿	River/Lake

HOW TO USE THIS GUIDE

Enjoying as much sun and fun on a vacation is everyone's dream. *Caribbean Sunseekers: Grenada* will help to make this dream come true. Your guide has been designed in three easy to use sections.

'Before You Go' is packed with detailed information on the island, its history, geography, people, culture, food and much more. 'Touring and Exploring Grenada' is a comprehensive itinerary covering the island with a series of useful and practical motoring or walking tours. Many places are off the beaten track and not on the usual tourist circuit. 'Traveller's Tips' arranged in alphabetical order for easy reference, lists practical information and useful advice to help you plan your vacation before you go and while you are there.

Distinctive margin symbols in the text and on maps, plus places to visit highlighted in bold enable the reader to find the most interesting places with ease.

Before You Go

Grenada, the Island of Spice, is the southernmost of the Windward Islands just 100 miles (160km) north of the coast of Venezuela, and one of the most beautiful. It has spectacular white sandy beaches, coral reefs, a rich history, a wonderfully relaxed atmosphere, great food and a people whose welcome is as warm as the year-round sunshine. Its many bays and sheltered anchorages make it one of the main yachting centres in the eastern Caribbean, its coral reefs and clear waters make it a mecca for divers, and its beaches and natural history are perfect for the holiday of a lifetime.

It is also an island that is taking tourism seriously. In 1994 there were 109,000 visitors and this is expected to rise to around 135,000 by 1997. Facilities are being improved all the time but not at the expense of the island's

A view of Queen's Park, St George's

natural beauty and charm. The consequences of the 1983 intervention are still having to be addressed, and the scars can still be seen around the island.

Grenada, however, is tackling these problems. It has embarked on an ambitious and ingenious clean up campaign to move derelict vehicles from the roadside into the sea to help establish artificial reefs, and legislation has already been introduced to control new hotels and other tourism developments. High rise buildings are not allowed, and developers are being encouraged to build new hotels and tourist accommodation away from the main tourist belt, not only to relieve pressure on St. George's and Grand Anse, but to open up new areas.

Everything possible that can be done, is being done, to ensure that Grenada remains an unspoiled, natural island.

GETTING TO GRENADA

By Air: There are international flights from North America, Europe and other parts of the Caribbean into Point Salines International Airport, which is 5 miles (8km) from St. George's.

Airlines flying into Grenada include Aereotuy, Air Europe, Airlines of Carriacou, American Airlines, BWIA, British Airways, Caledonian Airways, Canada 3000, Helenair and LIAT.

Carib Express which was launched in 1995 is based in Barbados, and operates the only jet service between the islands, flying 146s which require relatively short runways for take-off and landing. It flies between Barbados, Grenada, Dominica (Melville Hall), St. Lucia (Vigie), St. Vincent, as well as Tobago and Port of Spain.

American Airline offers flights from the United States to Grenada via its Caribbean hub in Puerto Rico. BWIA International provides direct services from New York, Toronto, Miami, and London via Trinidad and other Caribbean Islands.

Other North American carriers, including Air Canada, have flights to Barbados and Antigua that connect with LIAT and BWIA flights to and from Grenada. British Airways and British Caledonian provide direct services from London.

Charter services are provided by Aereotuy from Venezuela, Helenair from Grenada to neighbouring islands, Airlines of Carriacou to Carriacou, and Canada 3000.

All taxi fares from the airport are fixed by the Grenada Board of Tourism, and are usually given in US dollars. Always check the fare and which currency it is quoted in.

By Sea: A growing number of cruise lines now visit Grenada. These include American-Canadian, Carnival, Chandris, Clipper, Costa, Cunard, Epirotiki, Exploration, Exprinter, Hapah Lloyd, Holland America, Home Line, Kloster, NCL, North Star, Ocean Cruise Line, P&O, Premier, Regency, Royal Caribbean, Royal Cruise Line, Royal Viking, Salen, Seaburn and Sinbad.

GEOGRAPHY

Grenada is a three island state consisting of Grenada, Carriacou and Petit Martinique. The islands, part of the Windwards, are the southernmost in the Lesser Antilles, and lie in the eastern Caribbean. They cover an area of 344sq miles (892sq km).

Grenada is 21 miles (34km) north to south, 12 miles (19km) from east to west, oblong in shape, and covers an area of 120sq miles (311sq km). It has six parishes and five main towns. The capital, St. George's, is on the south-west coast and is also the island's main port, as well as one of the main yachting and boat charter centres in the eastern Caribbean. From Grenada there are a number of small islands — Bonaparte Rocks, Large Island, Rose Rock, Frigate Island, Saline Island and White Island — which lead to the Grenadines.

Carriacou, is the largest island of the southern Grenadines, and lies about 23 miles (37km) north, north-west, and covers an area of 13sq miles (34sq km). Petit Martinique, is a small volcanic cone, covering only 486 acres (194 hectares), and lies just off the north-east coast of Carriacou. Both islands are stunning with fabulous unspoilt beaches, coral reefs and turquoise clear waters. The islands have both white and black sand beaches. The white sand usually comes from tiny fragments of crushed shells and coral, while the black sand, which gets its colour from iron and manganese oxides, is finer.

There are many coral reefs around the islands, and the clear, warm waters are a mecca for divers, not just because of the rich marine life, but also because of the number of shipwrecks, casualties of the reefs and occasional tropical storms.

Grenada is a volcanic island with many extinct craters, and a

SUNSEEKER HOT SPOTS

ANTOINE ESTATE
rum distillery, beaches
page 92

CARRIACOU
lovely island, beaches, crafts
page 111

CONCORD FALLS
walks. scenery, wildlife
page 105

GRAND ANSE BAY
beaches, resorts, watersports
page 76

GRAND ETANG FOREST RESERVE
hikes, wildlife, tropical rain forest
page 108

GRAND ETANG LAKE
volcanic area, walks, wildlife, scenery
page 108

GRENVILLE
fishing town, beaches, historic sites
page 86

ROYAL MOUNT CARMEL WATERFALLS
scenery, wildlife, walks
page 86

SAUTEURS
Carib's Leap, Morne Fendue Plantation House
page 93

ST GEORGE'S
historic capital
page 60

central ridge of mountains running like a spine north to south. The waters surrounding Grenada are very deep suggesting that the island was created purely by volcanic activity, and was not part of a larger land mass that has since submerged.

Mount St. Catherine is the highest point at 2,756ft (840m), and when not capped by cloud, dominates the northern half of the island. The soils are volcanic and fertile, and there is some limestone in the north.

GEOLOGY

Geological investigation suggests the island was formed during a series of huge eruptions spanning back 25 million years. Originally the region was covered by a shallow sea and the layers of sand, silt and mud were gradually compressed into rock known as the Tufton Hall Formation. About 21 million years ago, a series of eruptions created the mountains in the north of the island. Levera Hill and Sugar Loaf Island were created by eruptions around 5 million years ago, about the time when the first eruptions took

place which created the south of the island. Lava flows in the south-west have been dated as 3.5 million years old, and this was probably the time of greatest volcanic activity. Most of the 'lahar' deposits in the south came from the sides of collapsing volcanoes, and as these mud slides travelled across the land, they tended to fill in craters and irregularities, giving the landscape a much more even aspect.

Major eruptions in the north continued until about 10,000 years ago, culminating in the creation of Mount St. Catherine, domes, such as Fedon's Camp and Mount Qua Qua, and the crater lakes of Antoine, Grand Etang, and the Carenage in St. George's. Apart from the hot springs, some of which emit sulphur, there is no evidence today of any volcanic activity on the island. Both Carriacou and Petit Martinique are the summits of submerged volcanic peaks, formed between 26 and 36 million years ago.

Diamond Island, a submarine volcano about 7 miles (11km) north of Grenada, is, however, one of the most active volcanoes

Preceding page: Grand Anse Bay

in the Lesser Antilles. Known locally as 'Kick 'em Jenny', it has erupted several times in the twentieth century, the last time in 1978, and the waters above it are often very rough.

The interior is mountainous with deep, steep-sided heavily forested lush valleys. The steeper slopes are to the west, while those to the east and south-east are more gently sloping. Most of the rivers and streams are short but fast running and provide much of the tap water for the population, and there are many waterfalls. The flow of rivers and waterfalls drops during the dry season months, and during the wet season, the volume of water is often so heavy that rivers overflow their banks. Water supplies are also provided by Grand Etang Lake, covering 36 acres (14 hectares) in the centre of the island. The lake has formed in the crater of an extinct volcano and is at an altitude of 1,740ft (530m).

HISTORY

The Amerindians

The first settlers on Grenada were Amerindian Siboneys, who travelled to the island from the mainland of South America around the first century AD. About 600 years later, the Arawaks, also Amerindians, arrived having followed the same path. They were a peaceful people who practised subsistence agriculture and fishing, and had no problems foraging for food because of the plentiful supply of wild fruits, vegetables and nuts. They were also skilled sailors and this perhaps explains why they were able to navigate their dug out canoes through the reef-strewn waters and reach Grenada safely. It is thought they arrived via Trinidad, and their first settlement is believed to have been on the south of the island close to the international airport. They lived in round huts with steep thatched roofs and walls made of plaited reeds, and grew maize, cassava, sweet potatoes and other crops in clearings, and as their numbers grew, the settlements spread around the island.

Their quiet lifestyle was shattered, however, by the arrival of the warlike Carib Indians who were spreading through the Caribbean. They may have first visited Grenada as early as AD100, but they arrived in force during the seventh century, and quickly wiped out most of the peaceable

BEACHES

Grenada has fabulous beaches, everything you ever dreamed of for a tropical island, golden sand, a fringe of tall palms for shade, and turquoise clear warm seas. Generally the best beaches are on the protected western coast. Beaches on the windier Atlantic Ocean coast tend to have choppier seas but offer excellent surfing and wind-surfing. Check locally for any swimming risks.

The Grenada Board of Tourism recommends the following beaches:
Grand Anse Beach, Morne Rouge Beach, La Sagesse Beach, Levera Beach and Bathway Beach.

TANNING SAFELY

The sun is very strong but sea breezes often disguise just how hot it is. If you are not used to the sun, take it carefully for the first two or three days, use a good sun screen with a factor of 15 or higher, and do not sunbathe during the hottest parts of the day. Wear sunglasses and a sun hat. Sunglasses will protect you against the glare, especially strong on the beach, and sun hats will protect your head.

If you spend a lot of time swimming or scuba diving, take extra care, as you will burn even quicker because of the combination of salt water and sun.

Calamine lotion and preparations containing aloe are both useful in combating sunburn.

A beach on the north-west coast

Arawaks, taking the survivors as slaves. They then dominated the island for almost 1,000 years. The Caribs lived in larger rectangular-shaped huts, again with thatched roofs and plaited reed walls. Several families often lived under the same roof, while the chieftain usually occupied the largest house in the village, although this was dwarfed by carbet, the village meeting place capable of holding more than 100 people. The Caribs were feared not only because of their fighting skills, but also because they were thought to be cannibals. It was rumoured that they ate their prisoners of war, but there is no evidence of cannibalism.

The Caribs were excellent hunters and they brought many innovations to the island. They discovered that the pulped root of the cassava tree produced a liquid called casareep, which was a preservative. Meat boiled in the liquid could be kept edible for indefinite periods, and this practice is the basis today of the famous Grenada pepper pot. Meat is put in the pot, casareep, peppers and spices are added and the liquid is then brought to the boil. Provided the liquid is brought to the boil each day, the meat retains its freshness, and as some of the contents of the pot

are eaten, new ingredients can be added. It is said that some of the island's pepper pots, contents and all, have been passed down through several generations and are still in use.

The First Europeans

Christopher Columbus was the first European to 'discover' Grenada. He sighted the island while aboard the Santa Maria on 15 August 1498, and although he did not land, he named it Concepción, despite the fact that other early European explorers referred to Grenada by its Amerindian name of 'Camerhogne'.

An attempt by the British to establish a trading post in 1609 at Megrin close to La Sagesse, failed when the settlers were driven out by the Caribs, and a similar attempt by the French in 1638 ended just as disastrously.

In 1650, the French governor of Martinique, Du Parquet, purchased Grenada from the Caribs and established the settlement of Port Louis with 200 people. The Carib chief Kaieroune received as payment only a few knives, axes, some glass beads, and two bottles of brandy. He soon realised they had been cheated and swore to drive the French from his land. Whenever the settlers left the safety of the settlement, they were attacked and killed by the Caribs. The French retaliated by bringing in extra troops, and gradually most of the Caribs were driven northwards, taking refuge in a fortified village. The village was overrun and most of the inhabitants slaughtered, but some men escaped and regrouped in the hills. The French sent to Martinique for reinforcements, while Caribs from other nearby islands arrived to continue the struggle.

The showdown came in 1651, when a force of 800 Caribs armed with clubs and bows and arrows, attacked the French in Fort George. Fort George was built in 1706, therefore that area was called some other name at the time (1650). The French armed with cannon, rifles and pistols massacred them. The few surviving Caribs fled but were pursued by the French to the very northern tip of the island. Finally cornered, the Caribs leapt to their deaths into the sea rather than be taken prisoner.

The incident provoked fury among Caribs on other islands and also those who were still living in hiding in Grenada. They swore revenge, and over the next few years several raids took place

in which Frenchmen were attacked and killed. The French responded harshly, hunting out and killing any Carib they could find, and by 1700 all but a handful had been slain.

Traces of their culture still remain, however, with rock paintings, burial sites, pottery and many words of Amerindian origin. In 1665 the island was sold to the French West India Company but was taken over by the French Crown in 1674, and the island stayed in French hands until 1762 when it was captured by the British — without a shot being fired. A year later it was formally ceded to Britain by the Treaty of Paris, and the first British Colonial Government of Grenada was established by George III. In 1767 the entire island was declared a free port by the British government, which saw a rapid expansion in trade over the next 30 years.

The first French settlers planted tobacco as their main crop, and then switched to indigo and livestock, but in 1702 sugar cane was introduced from South America, and over the next 100 years it transformed the island's economy. Growing cane economically was only possible with lots of cheap labour so the slave trade flourished. In 1714

Shopping

Shops are usually open between 8am-4pm Monday to Friday, and from 8am-1pm on Saturday. Fodland on Lagoon Road in St. George's, and Gittens Drug Mart in Grand Anse stay open until 8pm.

Grenada, Carriacou and Petit Martinique offer fine batik and handscreen printed fabrics and clothes. Hats and visors woven from green palms make useful and interesting souvenirs, as do spice baskets filled with the island's produce. Other interesting things to buy include locally produced perfumes, natural extracts of spices, jellies, preserves and sweets, and hand crafted wood, wicker and straw items. All of these are available from the National Handicrafts Centre. The main shopping areas are in St. George's around the Carenage, Market Square and Granby Street, and in the Grand Anse resort area. The island boasts many fine artists and their works can be viewed and purchased from galleries, and are often displayed along the Carenage.

The market stalls near the pier in St George's, selling spices and other local products

cotton, coffee and cocoa were also introduced. Tobacco was produced until the end of the nineteenth century, coffee until the 1920s, and cotton was exported for the last time in 1981.

St. George's was originally settled by the French in 1705 who called it Port Royale, and work on Fort George started the following year. The town's name changed to St. George's when control passed from the French to the British. The town was destroyed by fire which swept through the wooden buildings in 1771, and the town suffered the same fate again after rebuilding in 1775. As a result, a law was passed banning the construction of any building not built of brick or stone and covered with tiles, and this accounts for the remarkable city one can see today, especially the fine old red tile roofed warehouses along the waterfront. The law did not prevent more damage in 1792 when fire struck again, and a third of the town was destroyed.

The French sided with the Americans during the 1775-6 War of Independence, and this led to war between France and Britain. In 1778, a French fleet which had been harrassing the British navy off the North American coast sailed into the Caribbean. For a time, the French were trapped in harbour in Martinique because of a Royal Navy blockade, but they broke out in 1779, sailed south to St. Vincent and captured the island from the British. They then moved on Grenada, landing troops up the coast so that they were able to launch a surprise attack on St. George's from inland. The British surrendered and the island was in French hands again until 1783, when the Treaty of Versailles drew a line through the northern tip of Carriacou in the Grenadines, and gave the islands to the south of it, including Grenada, back to Britain. That line still marks the boundary between the three island state of Grenada, and the state of St. Vincent and the Grenadines to the north.

As part of the British expansion, large numbers of slaves were brought from Africa to work in the many sugar plantations. In 1795 the slaves and 'free coloured' rebelled against British rule, largely enboldened by the anti-slavery stance taken by the French on Martinique. The rebellion was led by Julien Fedon, a French planter, and supported by Martinique. During 1795 and 1796 many plantation owners were killed as well as the lieutenant governor. The 14-month long rebellion was finally crushed by a large force led by Sir Ralph Abercromby, and many of the ring leaders publicly hanged in St. George's. Fedon escaped capture and disappeared. But, the seeds of emancipation had been sown although it was not until 1834 that slavery was finally abolished.

In 1795 the West Indian Regiment was founded manned by West Indians with British officers. It originally consisted of two battalions raised in South Carolina and St. Vincent. By 1800, there were 12 battalions stationed throughout the Caribbean, the Regiment had a distinguished record until its disbandment in 1927. In 1914, the 3rd Grenadian contingent of the Regiment sailed from the Carenage to fight in the trenches of Europe during World War I.

Even after Emancipation, all newly freed slaves over the age of 6 were required to be 'apprenticed' for 4 years, during which time they had to work without pay for their former owners for three quarters of their working week. As more and more slaves gained their freedom, there was a need for new workers, and a system of indentured labour

was introduced. The system had started in the seventeenth century when mainly English and Irish workers were employed as 'indentured servants'. They usually worked for 3 to 7 years for board and lodging but no pay, in the expectation of receiving a grant of land at the end of their service. After the Industrial Revolution in Europe, however, this labour was no longer available, and after Emancipation, large numbers of Portugese, Maltese and West African indentured labourers were brought in. Many sugar estates, however, could not compete with Spanish plantations still employing slave labour, and were forced to close. In 1857 indentured Indian labour allowed some of these estates to re-open, but there was a shift in production away from sugar cane to cocoa. Emancipated slaves also took to growing cocoa in clearings in the forests, and over the next few decades huge tracts of upland forest were cleared. In 1843 nutmegs were introduced into Grenada from Indonesia, and when the Indonesian plantations were devastated by disease 10 years later, the world price shot up and there was large scale

Following page: Nutmegs, once a lucrative crop in the island economy

planting on Grenada. Nutmeg trees, however, take a long time to grow, and there were significant exports until 1881. The practice of indentured labour continued until 1917.

Today nutmegs, cocoa and bananas, which have only been grown as an economic crop since the 1950s, are the island's main agricultural export. Tourism is also a major income earner and developing rapidly.

Grenada had an elected House of Assembly between 1763 and 1876 (except for the period 1779-83) when it voted to disband itself, and then from 1876 to 1924 it was a Crown Colony governed from London, and between 1885 and 1958 Grenada was the seat of the Windward Islands government.

In 1924, largely thanks to the campaigning of Theophilus Albert Marryshow, 'The Father of Federation', the first limited elections for a Legislative Council were held. Born in 1885, he was editor of the S*t. George's Chronicle* by the age of 26, and he helped found *The West Indian* in 1915 which, as editor, became his campaign mouthpiece. He was passionate in his calls for

democratically elected government and a Federation of the British West Indies. Despite the campaigning, however, it was not until 1951 that all adults got the vote.

In 1958 Grenada joined the West Indies Federation, and when the Federation ended in 1962, the island attempted to establish a federation with the other Windward Islands, as well as Barbados and the Leeward Islands. On 3 March 1967 Grenada became a self-governing state in association with the United Kingdom, and in the general election in August that year, the Grenada United Labour Party (GULP) defeated the Grenada National Party (GNP), and took office under the premiership of Eric M. Gairy, one of the pioneers of the country's trade union movement and founder of the GULP. He was knighted in 1977.

Grenada became an independent nation on 7 February 1974, becoming a member of the Commonwealth and the United Nations. The transition to independence, however, was marred by strikes and opposition to the continued

Preceding page: The Sugar Loaf from Levera Bay

premiership of Gairy. The socialist New Jewel Movement (NJM), a coalition of opposition parties and opponents to the GULP, was formed. It incorporated the JEWEL group, which stood for Joint Action for Education, Welfare and Liberation, and had been founded by Unison Whiteman.

The NJM succeeded in reducing the ruling party's majority in parliament in the 1976 elections. On 13 March 1979, while the Prime Minister was on a visit to the United States, the NJM staged a near bloodless coup and on 29 March, proclaimed itself the People's Revolutionary Government, naming their 35 year-old lawyer leader Maurice Bishop as the new Prime Minister. He was not elected to this office, although he had been the democratically elected Leader of the Opposition for the previous 3 years. The former Prime Minister did not return to Grenada until January 1984.

The new left wing government, which faced opposition from most western countries, announced a programme to rebuild the economy, but its rule ended in October 1983 during an internal power struggle in which Bishop, ten members of his cabinet, and many civilians were killed.

The coup leaders declared a Revolutionary Military Council, but at the request of the Governor General Sir Paul Scoon a US and Caribbean-led force took over the island, arrested the coup leaders and returned power to the governor general. The peacekeeping force remained on the island until 1985 although constitutional government had been restored and general elections held the previous December. The New National Party led by Herbert A. Blaize, who had been premier in the 1960s, won the election and took office in December 1984. In 1989 although still Prime Minister, he lost the leadership of the party, and on 31 August 1989 launched The National Party. At its first convention on 17 December 1989, he was elected the party's Political Leader, but he died 2 days later.

Ben Jones, a long time friend of Blaize, was appointed Prime Minister in the interim by the Governor General. New elections were held on 13 March 1990 when The National Party were voted out of office, and the National Democratic Congress led by Nicholas Brathwaite, became the Governing party. He had previously been appointed Chairman of the Interim

Government by Governor General Sir Paul Scoon following the 1983 intervention.

Although he resigned as leader of his party in 1994, he remained as Prime Minister and was appointed a Member of the Privy Council in 1991. The current Governor General is Sir Reginald Palmer, who was sworn in on 6 August 1992. Grenadian born, he retired from public service in 1980 after a distinguished career in education.

CLIMATE

The island has an average year round temperature of 29°C (84°F), but can rise to 32°C+ (90°F) and higher during August and November, and fall to 18°C (65°F) overnight in the mountains. Prevailing onshore winds provide welcome cooling breezes and reduce humidity levels. The sun rises and sets quite quickly so dawn and dusk do not last long, but the sunsets, as the sun sinks below the horizon out at sea, are usually fantastic. Sunrise is generally around 6am, and sunset about 6pm. During the summer there are about 13 hours of daylight and about 11 hours during the winter. These winds are strongest along the eastern (windward) coastline.

Rainfall varies from about 60 inches (150cm) around the coast, to more than 150 inches (380cm) in the mountainous interior. The Point Salines area on the southern tip of the island has the least rainfall and is the most arid. The rainy season lasts from June to December with November usually the wettest month. Tropical showers, however, can occur at any time of the year, although the dry season officially extends from January to May. Grenada is south of the main hurricane belt but has been hit three times in its recorded history. On 22 September 1955 Hurricane Janet came ashore, the first time in living memory that the island had been hit by a hurricane. The 130mph (209kph) winds claimed approximately 114 lives, destroyed St. George's 850ft (259m) long pier and customs sheds, and caused widespread damage around the island, especially in the parish of St. Patrick and on Carriacou and Petit Martinique, which all bore the brunt of the storm. Grenada was also hit by tropical storms in 1979 and 1980 but there was considerably less damage caused.

Preceding page: Splitting cocoa pods

Carriacou and Petit Martinique enjoys if anything, an even better climate with year-round good weather, lower rainfall and balmy sea breezes.

THE PEOPLE

Most of the population of 96,000 is descended from African slaves, although there are also the descendents of East Indians brought to the islands as indentured labourers to replace the freed slaves, as well as the descendents of British and French settlers, and more recent immigrants from North America and Europe. Most of the population is Roman Catholic although many other denominations are represented including Anglican, Methodist and Seventh-Day Adventist.

While English is the official language, a form of patois is still widely spoken, especially by older people, and visitors will find it almost impossible to understand. The patois has retained many words of Old English and French Creole, and adopted and adapted scores of others from the various languages brought to the island by the many nationalities over the last 350 years.

CULTURE

Grenadians love to sing, dance and play music. It is in their blood, and this all comes together every year in Carnival. Although Carnival was celebrated before Emancipation in 1834, it was a subdued affair because slaves and 'free coloureds' were not allowed to take part. Afterwards it became more of a 'Festival of Protest', and incorporated other expressions of protest.

The festival of Cannes Brulee (Burnt Cane) was held in the eighteenth century to mark the end of the harvest, but after Emancipation it became part of the August 1st Emancipation Day celebrations symbolising the harsh treatment meted out to the slaves. Around the 1860s the festival, or Canboulay as it had become known, was held on the eve of Carnival, and today, the two have merged completely, and the true spirit of Carnival reigns supreme.

It is a time for music, dancing, partying and, of course, calypso, which can trace its roots back to West African traditional songs. The word calypso is thought to come from the West African word *kaiso*, which means well done.

Grenadian-born Slinger Francisco, known as The Mighty

Sparrow, is regarded by most as the 'Father of Modern Calypso'. He won his first calypso crown in 1956, and has performed around the world. The essence of calypso is topicality, highlighting or satirising political and social issues with clever lyrics and catchy melodies.

Grenada has a number of fine dance and folk groups. The National Folk Group draws its artists from four of the island's most outstanding groups — the Cariawa Folk Group from the parish of St. Patrick, the Spice Island Youth-quake, from the parish of St. John, the Veni-Vwai La Grenada Dance Company and the Impulse Dance Company both from the parish of St. George. Although all the performers are amateurs, the group bursts with talent and has made a number of international appearances.

The Cariawa Folk Group specialises in folk songs and folk opera, especially in patois, and have toured the UK. The Veni-Vwai La Grenada Dance Company have choreographed new dance routines based on traditional folk dances, and the Spice Island Youth-quake, concentrate mainly on religious and folk songs, while the Impulse Dance Company is noted for modern dance, folk and classical ballet.

Traditional dances include the bongo, traditionally performed when someone has died and intended to help the soul travel safely to heaven; the stick fight (kalinda), also a dance for the dead to speed them through purgatory; and the colourful Bele, the West Indian version of the Lancers and Quadrille, and very similar except that it incorporates traditional African steps. Carriacou is also noted for its long dance tradition, and this is dealt with in greater detail in the Carriacou section on page 111.

Grenada has also produced and adopted many artists of note. Elinus Cato, born in St. Patrick in 1933, is one of the island's most popular artists, and in 1985 his painting *People at Work* was presented to Queen Elizabeth II to commemorate her visit to Grenada. He concentrates now on landscapes.

Jackie Miller, is a self-taught artist whose works, in a variety of mediums, are sold internationally. Michael Paryag was born in Sauteurs in 1969, and was

Facing page: A spice mill in Gouyave

encouraged to paint by his mother, a talented amateur water colourist. His works of island scenes and life have been sold internationally.

Joseph Rome is a very talented sculptor who learnt his craft using materials available naturally, such as tree bark and clay which he dug from the ground. He still uses natural materials such as red sand white cedar and mahogany from the local forests.

Winston Fleary, has done more than most to preserve the island's heritage and traditions, especially the Big Drum Culture on Carriacou. He has led tours to the United States and Britain and has produced acclaimed stage presentations around the world featuring the island's dance and music.

Trish Bethany arrived as a visitor on the island in the late 1960s and was so captivated by it that she gave up her job and stayed. She became a teacher while starting out on her artistic career. At first she photographed scenes then painted what she had photographed, but now she paints 'self generating images', and her work is highly collectable.

Island galleries include Yellow Poi Art Gallery, Cross Street, Frangipani, The Carenage, Creation Arts and Crafts, Carenage, and Tikal, Young Street, all in St. George's, and Rose Andall Watercolours at Fort Jeudy.

FOLKLORE

Folklore abounds on Grenada and many of the tales have been passed down by mouth from generation to generation. The stories were a means of preserving old myths and traditions, and incorporated African folkore, philosophy and moral tales.

Many of the stories, however, tell of malevolent spirits roaming the countryside at night, and are full of symbolism about slavery, oppression and hardship.

There is the evil Mama Maladie, the mother of diseases, who tries to trick her way into your home by imitating the sound of a crying child. There is also the Lig-ah-rou, a word derived from the French Creole for a werewolf. This beast though can fly, and squeeze through a keyhole in order to suck the blood of its victims, although it can only be out during the hours of darkness. The defence, according to legend is to place a pile of sand outside your door, as the Lig-ah-rou must count every grain before entering. This should take until dawn. As the beast can only fly if it takes off its skin, you should look out for this and sprinkle it with salt. Then when the werewolf returns and puts his skin back on, you will be able to spot him because he will be constantly scratching due to the irritating salt.

There are lots of other evil spirits, including La-jab-less, a skeletal demoness with a cloven hoof for one of her feet, who literally frightens wayward husbands to death.

Carnival features bizarrely-dressed men portraying 'Jab-jab', the molasses devil, symbolising slavery.

THE ECONOMY

Agriculture and tourism are the island's most important economic sectors, with fishing and agricultural products becoming more important. Agriculture is largely dependent on many small landowners growing a large number of different crops. Many of the smallholdings are in the mountains in clearings or on terraces and are unsuitable for mechanical cultivation. Main agricultural crops are bananas, cocoa, nutmeg and mace and much of the production is handled by co-operatives. The island's cocoa is of a high quality and accounts for about 38 per cent of agricultural export earnings. Mace is not only used as a spice, it is sold worldwide to pharmaceutical and perfumery companies. Bananas were cultivated in earnest after the 1955 hurrricane when the cocoa and nutmeg groves were devastated, and are now a major crop. Grenada gets its name as the Island of Spice, because it is also a major producer of cinnamon, cloves, allspice, pimento and tumeric (sold locally as 'saffron'). These spices and others such as bay, vanilla, sapote, ginger and tonka bean can be bought in the local markets, and tasted in many of the island's dishes.

Lime juice, copra and other coconut products have also become economically significant as exports, as have a wide range of tropical fruits and vegetables, such as mangoes, passion fruit, guavas, tamarind and citrus. Staple crops such as tomatoes, peas, sweet potatoes, pumpkins, squash and maize are largely grown for home consumption. Forestry for teak and mahogany exports is also important.

There are about 2,000 full and part time fishermen and 600 'M' registered boats permitted for fishing. Main species landed are

A NOTE OF
WARNING
THE MANCHINEEL

The manchineel, which can be found on many beaches, has a number of effective defensive mechanisms which can prove very painful. Trees vary from a few feet to more than 30ft (9m) in height, and have widely spreading, deep forked boughs with small, dark green leaves and yellow stems, and fruit like small, green apples. If you examine the leaves carefully without touching them, you will notice a small pin-head sized raised dot at the junction of leaf and leaf stalk. The apple-like fruit is poisonous, and sap from the tree causes very painful blisters. It is so toxic, that early Caribs are said to have dipped their arrow heads in it before hunting trips. Sap is released if a leaf or branch is broken, and more so after rain. Avoid contact with the tree, do not sit under it, or on a fallen branch, and do not eat the fruit. If you do get sap on your skin, run into the sea and wash it off as quickly as possible.

tuna, billfish, flying fish and dorado, mostly in November and December and June and July. Fishermen from around Gouyave use wooden hulled canoes and motor powered pirogues, and lines up to 3½ miles (6km) long. Bottom dwelling species such as grouper, snapper and rockfish are usually caught between June and November, while inshore seine net fishing for scad and sardines, takes place throughout the year. Shellfish are also an important landing. There are six fish markets in Grenada but most is still sold from the boat, or direct to buyers for export.

Tourism is growing, thanks to much improved facilities for long haul jets and cruise ships. Other industries include rum distilling, brewing, food and fish canning, copra processing, clothing, furniture, paint and cigarette manufacture, soap making, flour milling, animal feeds and handicrafts.

Loofas are a fruit and they can be seen growing around the island

FLORA AND FAUNA

The lush vegetation and animal life are part of the island's great charm and there is a year-round growing season. Almost all the land that could be cultivated was utilised by the plantations, and great efforts have been made by recent governments to protect and conserve the remaining forest reserves. The Grand Etang Reserve alone now covers more than 3,800 acres (1,520 hectares).

Most of the island has a volcanic landscape and palms of all descriptions can be found everywhere, especially in the central mountains. The highest altitudes are covered with dwarf woodlands, but in the rainforests south of Mount Qua Qua, the trees can tower 100ft (30m) and more into the canopy. At slightly lower altitudes there is montane thicket with trees of enormous girth and few ground shrubs, although a thick carpet of ferns, grasses and small orchids, as well as some creepers. Because of the humidity there is also plenty of moss.

As most of the orginal forest growth was cleared for the plantations, much of what can be seen today is second growth with many species not originally found on the island.

Almost wherever one looks, however, there is greenery and lush growth. There are giant ferns and bamboos, bananas, coconut groves, hanging breadfruit, mango, nutmeg, cocoa and pawpaw, and the most stunning array of spectacularly coloured flowering plants from giant African tulip trees festooned with scarlet blossom to tiny orchids. Bougainvillea flowers everywhere, there are scores of varieties of hibiscus, frangipani and poinsettia. There are heliconia, also known as the lobster plant, bird of paradise flowers and anthurium everywhere. The flamboyant tree is also known as the tourist tree because it bursts into bloom during the summer and is a blaze of colour.

Along the coast you can find mangrove swamps, especially around Levera in the north, and along river estuaries in the south. There are marsh woodlands and inland there are breathtaking walks through tropical rain forests of mahogany, teak and saman (also known as the rain tree), and blue mahoe.

Beach morning glory with its array of pink flowers is found on many beaches, and is important because its roots help prevent sand drift. The plant also produces nectar from glands in the base of its leaf stalks which attract ants, and it is thought this evolution has occurred so that the ants will discourage any leaf-nibbling predators. Other beach plants include seagrape and the manchineel, which should be treated with caution (see feature box on page 34).

Of course, the sea teems with brilliantly coloured fish and often, even more spectacularly coloured coral and marine plants. Even if you just float upside down in the water with a face mask on, you will be able to enjoy many of the beautiful underwater scenes, but the best way to see things is by scuba diving, snorkelling or taking a trip in one of the many glass bottomed boats.

There are scores of different multi-coloured corals that make up the reefs offshore. There are hard and soft corals and only one, the fire coral, poses a threat to swimmers and divers because if touched it causes a stinging skin rash. Among the more spectacular corals are deadman's fingers, staghorn, brain coral and seaf-ans, and there are huge sea anemones and sponges, while tropical fish species include the parrotfish, blue tang surgeonfish, tiny but aggressive damselfish, angelfish and brightly coloured wrasse. There are reefs along the northern, eastern and southern coasts, especially off Levera Bay.

Coastal swamps also provide a rich habitat for wildlife. Tiny tree crabs and burrowing edible land crabs scurry around in the mud trapped in the roots of mangrove trees just above water level. Herons, egrets, pelicans and often frigatebirds roost in the higher branches. The mangrove cuckoo shares the lower branches with belted kingfishers.

Inland, gardens are generally a blaze of colour with flowers in bloom year round, growing alongside exotic vegetables like yam, sweet potato, and dasheen. Flowering plants include the flamboyant tree with their brilliant red flowers which burst into bloom in early summer, and long dark brown seed pods, up to 2ft (½m) which can be used as rattles when the seeds have dried out inside. Occasionally flamboyants have yellow blossom but this is extremely rare. Bougainvillea, Grenada's national flower, grows everywhere and seems to be in bloom year round in a host of different colours, In fact, the colour does not come from petals but the plant's bract-like leaves which surround the small petalless flowers.

There are yellow and purple allamandas, poinsettia, hibiscus, anthurium and multi-coloured flowers of the ixora. The leaves of the travellers palm spread out like a giant open fan, and the tree got its name because the fan was believed to point from south to north. However it rarely does.

The flowers attract hummingbirds like the doctorbird, as well as the carib grackle, a strutting, starling-like bird with a paddle-shaped tail, and friendly bananaquit. You can also spot tree lizards, and the larger geckos which hunt at night.

Along roadsides and hedgerows in the countryside, you can see the vinelike caralita, calabash with its gourd-like fruits, tamarind and distinctive star-shaped leaves of the castor bean, whose seeds when crushed yield castor oil.

Areas of scrubland have their own flora or fauna, with plants bursting into colour following the first heavy rains after the dry

Roadside vendors selling spices and nutmeg jelly

A NOTE OF
WARNING
PEPPER SAUCE – HOT OR HOTTER?

On most tables you will find a bottle of pepper sauce. It usually contains a blend of several types of hot pepper, spices and vinegar, and should be treated cautiously. Try a little first before splashing it all over your food, as these sauces range from hot to unbearable.

If you want to make your own hot pepper sauce, take four ripe hot peppers, one teaspoon each of oil, ketch-up and vinegar and a pinch of salt, blend together into a liquid, and bottle.

season. There are century plants, with their prickly, sword like leaves, which grow for up to 20 years before flowering. The yellow flower stalk grows at a tremendous rate for several days and can reach 20ft (6m) high, but having bloomed once the whole plant then dies. Other typical scrubland vegetation includes aloe, acacia, prickly pear and several species of cactus. Fiddlewood provides hard timber for furniture, highly coloured variagated crotons, the white flowered, aromatic frangipani and sea island cotton, which used to provide the very finest cotton. Scrub vegetation also plays host to birds such as the mockingbird, ground dove,

kingbird and grassquit, and it is the ideal habitat for lizards.

The rain forests provide the most prolific vegetation with mahogany trees with their fascinating black and red seeds, much used for necklaces. There are magnificent swathes of giant ferns, towering bamboo groves, enormous air plants, and a host of flowering or variegated plants such as heliconia, philodendron and wild fuchsia. There are balsa wood trees, the world's lightest wood, the flowering vine marcgravia, and the prolific mountain cabbage palm, and among the foliage and flowers you can find hummingbirds and parrots.

The animal life on the island is

not diverse and there are few large animals. There is the mona monkey, a small, long-tailed primate from West Africa, which was introduced by slaves, and can be seen around the Grand Etang and upper slopes of Mount St. Catherine. There is the nine banded armadillo, iguana, and two species of opossum, including the manicou, which lives in trees, forages over huge areas at night, and is not averse to rooting through trash cans for any delicacies. There are eleven known species of bats. The agouti is now extinct on the island, and it is thought that the last of these rodents died around the time of Hurricane Janet.

There are also piping frogs found in the woodlands and highlands, and giant toads which croak loudly all night, geckos, lizards and snakes such as the white headed worm snake, tree boa, Boddaert's snake and the cribo, a constrictor. None of the island's snakes are poisonous.

Mongooses, which grow up to 2ft (½m) in length including tail, were said to have been first introduced to the islands from Jamaica via Burma, to kill rats gnawing at the sugar cane.

Lumbering sea turtles also come ashore at night between May and September to lay their eggs in the sand. There are butterflies and less attractive insects such as mosquitoes, ants and sand flies.

There is, however, a remarkable rich and colourful native bird life. There are more than 150 native species including mangrove cuckoos, hummingbirds, tanagers, ibis, mockingbirds, herons, egrets and many others, and more than 100 species of migrants, who pass through between their breeding grounds in North America and over-wintering grounds in the Caribbean or South America. Levera Pond is one of the best spots for sighting migrant birds.

Offshore you may sight the magnificent frigatebird, easily recognisable by its size, long black 7ft (2m) wing span, forked tail and apparent effortless ability to glide on the winds. There are brown booby birds, named by sailors from the Spanish word for 'fool' because they were so easy to catch. Pelicans which look so ungainly on land, yet are so acrobatic in the air, are common, as are laughing gulls and royal terns. Several species of sandpiper can usually be seen scurrying around at the water's edge.

There are no parrots on the island even though they are found on the neighbouring island of St. Vincent. Parrots were recorded by visitors in the early seventeenth century, but it is thought they might have become extinct after the introduction of the mona monkey which would have raided their nests for the eggs. The chicken hawk, or broadwing hawk, is the most common bird of prey. Also of interest is the rusty-tailed flycatcher, scaly-breasted thrasher, black-billed thrush, Lesser Antillean bullfinch and Lesser Antillean tanager which are only found in Grenada, the Grenadines or Lesser Antilles.

The rarest bird is the Grenada Dove, found only on the island. There are believed to be less than 100 in the wild, and despite measures to protect it, it is in danger of extinction because of hunting and habitat destruction. Special reserves have been established to help protect it. The Ramier Dove and the nine banded Armadillo are part of the country's National Coat of Arms. Also endangered and protected are the Grenada hookbilled kite and the Euler's flycatcher.

If you are really interested in bird watching pack a small pair of binoculars. The new mini-binoculars are ideal for island bird watching, because the light is normally so good that you will get a clear image despite the small object lens.

Binoculars will also be useful if you want to go whale spotting. Humpback whales winter in the warm waters, and they used to be hunted from a whaling station which operated from Glover Island, off Grenada.

As most of the plants, fruits, vegetables and spices will be new to the first time visitor, the following brief descriptions are offered.

Bananas are one of the island's most important exports, thus their nickname 'green gold', and grow everywhere. There are three types of banana plant. The banana that we normally buy in supermarkets originated in Malaya and were introduced into the Caribbean in the early sixteenth century by the Spanish. The large bananas, or plantains, originally came from southern India, and are largely used in cooking. They are often fried and served as an accompaniment to fish and meat. The third variety is the red banana, which is not grown commercially, but which can be seen around the island. Most banana plantations cover only a few acres and are worked by the owner or tenant, although there are still some very large holdings. A banana produces a crop about every 9

Nutmeg factory at Gouyave

months, and each cluster of flowers grows into a hand of bananas. A bunch can contain up to 20 hands of bananas, with each hand having up to 20 individual fruit.

Although they grow tall, bananas are not trees but herbacious plants which die back each year. Once the plant has produced fruit, a shoot from the ground is cultivated to take its place, and the old plant dies. Bananas need a lot of attention, and island farmers will tell you

Facing page: Schoolchildren on Grenada are always friendly to visitors

that there are not enough hours in a day to do everything that needs to be done. The crop needs fertilising regularly, leaves need cutting back, and you will often see the fruit inside blue tinted plastic bags, which protect it from insect and bird attack, the sun's rays, and speed up maturation.

The **Bay tree** is a native of the Windward Islands, a member of the Laurel family and can grow to a height of 30ft (9m). The leaves are gently crushed for their oil which is used in the perfume industry. The oil is also used to produce a special rum which is said to have antiseptic properties, while the leaves are used in cooking.

Breadfruit was introduced to the Caribbean by Captain Bligh in 1793. He brought 1,200 breadfruit saplings from Tahiti aboard the *Providence*, and these were first planted in Jamaica and St. Vincent, and then quickly spread throughout the islands. It was Bligh's attempts to bring in young breadfruit trees that led to the mutiny on the *Bounty* 4 years earlier. Bligh was given the command of the 215 ton *Bounty* in 1787 and was ordered to take the breadfruit trees from Tahiti to the West Indies where they were to be used to provide cheap

food for the slaves. The ship had collected its cargo and had reached Tonga when the crew under Fletcher Christian mutinied. The crew claimed that Bligh's regime was too tyranical, and he and eighteen members of the crew who stayed loyal to him, were cast adrift in an open boat. The cargo of breadfruit was dumped overboard. Bligh, in a remarkable feat of seamanship, navigated the boat for 3,600 miles (5,796km) until making landfall on Timor in the East Indies. Some authorities have claimed that it was the breadfruit tree cargo that sparked the mutiny, as each morning the hundreds of trees in their heavy containers had to be carried on deck, and then carried down into the hold at nightfall. It might have proved just too much for the already overworked crew.

Whatever the reason for the mutiny, the breadfruit is a cheap carbohydrate-rich food, although pretty tasteless when boiled. It is best eaten fried, baked or roasted over charcoal. The slaves did not like them at first, but the tree spread and can now be found almost everywhere. It has large dark, green leaves, and the large green fruits can weigh 10 to 12lb (4 to 5kgm). The falling fruits explode with a loud bang and splatter pulpy contents over a large distance. It is said that no one goes hungry when the breadfruit is in season.

Calabash trees are native to the Caribbean and have huge gourd like fruits which are very versatile when dried and cleaned. They can be used as water containers and bowls, bailers for boats, and as lanterns. Juice from the pulp is boiled into a concentrated syrup and used to treat coughs and colds, and the fruit is said to have many other medicinal uses.

Cinnamon comes from bark of an evergreen tree, also related to the laurel. The bark is rolled into 'sticks' and dried, and then ground or sold in small pieces. It is used as a spice, for flavouring, and adds a sweet, aromatic flavour to many dishes. Oil from the bark is used to flavour sweets, soaps, toothpastes and liqueurs, while oil from the leaves is used in perfumes.

Cocoa is another important crop, and its Latin name *theobroma* means 'food of the gods'. A cocoa tree can produce several thousand flowers a year, but only a fraction of these will develop into seed bearing pods. It is the heavy orange pods that hang from the cocoa tree which contain the beans which contain the seeds that produce cocoa and chocolate. The beans, containing a sweet, white sap that protects the seeds, are split open and kept in trays to ferment. This process takes up to 8 days and the seeds must be kept at a regular temperature to ensure the right flavour and aroma develops. The seeds are then dried. In the old days people used to walk barefoot over the beans to polish them to enhance their appearance. Today, the beans are crushed to extract cocoa butter, and the remaining powder is cocoa. Real chocolate is produced by mixing cocoa powder, cocoa butter and sugar.

You can buy cocoa balls or rolls, like fat chocolate fingers, in the markets which make a delicious drink. Each ball is the size of a large cherry. Simply dissolve the ball in a pan of boiling water, allow to simmer and then add salt, sugar and milk or cream, for a rich chocolate drink. Each ball will make about four mugs of chocolate.

Coconut palms are everywhere and should be treated with caution. Anyone who has heard the '*whoosh*' of a descending coconut, and leapt to safety, knows how scary the sound is. Very few people do get injured by falling coconuts and that is a near miracle in view of the tens of thousands of palms all over the island. However it is not a good idea to picnic in a coconut grove!

Coconut trees are incredibly hardy, able to grow in sand and even when regularly washed by salty sea water. They can also survive long periods without rain. Their huge leaves, up to 20ft (6m) long in mature trees, drop down during dry spells so a smaller surface area is exposed to the sun which reduces evaporation. Coconut palms can grow up to 80ft (24m) tall, and produce up to 100 seeds a year. The seeds are the second largest in the plant kingdom, and these fall when ripe.

The coconut traditionally bought in greengrocers, is the seed with its layer of coconut surrounded by a hard shell. This shell is then surrounded by a layer of copra, a fibrous material, and this is covered by a large green husk. The seed and protective coverings can weigh 30lb (13kgm) and more. The seed and casing is waterproof, drought proof and able to float, and this explains why coconut palms which originated in the Pacific and Indian Oceans, are now found throughout the Caribbean — the seeds literally floated across the seas.

The coconut palm is extremely versatile. The leaves can be used as thatch for roofing, or cut into strips and woven into mats and baskets, while the husks yield coir, a fibre resistant to salt water and ideal for ropes and brushes and brooms. Green coconuts contain a delicious thirst-quenching 'milk', and the coconut 'meat' can be eaten raw, or baked in ovens for 2 days before being sent to processing plants where the oil is extracted. Coconut oil is used in cooking, soaps, synthetic rubber and even in hydraulic brake fluid.

As you drive around the island, you will see groups of men and women splitting the coconuts in half with machetes preparing them for the ovens. You might also see halved coconut shells spaced out on the corrugated tin roofs of some homes. These are being dried before being sold to the copra processing plants.

Dasheen is one of the crops known as 'ground provisions' in the islands, the others being potatoes, yams, eddo and tannia. The last two are close relatives of dasheen, and all are members of

Facing page: Westerhall

the aroid family, some of the world's oldest cultivated crops. Dasheen with its 'elephant ear' leaves, and eddo grow from a corm which when boiled thoroughly can be used like potato, and the young leaves of either are used to make callaloo, a spinach-like soup. Both dasheen and eddo are thought to have come from China or Japan but tannia is native to the Caribbean, and its roots can be boiled, baked or fried.

Guava is common throughout the islands, and the aromatic, pulpy fruit is also a favourite with birds who then distribute its seeds. The fruit bearing shrub can be seen on roadsides and in gardens, and it is used to make a wide range of products from jelly to 'cheese', a paste made by mixing the fruit with sugar. The fruit which range from a golf ball to a tennis ball in size, is a rich source of vitamin A and contains lots more vitamin C than citrus fruit.

Mango can be delicious if somewhat messy to eat. It originally came from India but is now grown throughout the Caribbean and found wherever there are people. Young mangoes can be stringy and unappetising, but ripe fruit from mature trees which grow up to 50ft (15m) and more, are usually delicious, and can be eaten raw or cooked. The juice is a great reviver in the morning, and the fruit is often used to make jams and other preserves. The wood of the mango is often used by boatbuilders.

Nutmeg trees are found on all the islands but Grenada is one of the world's top producers, although the price farmers get has crashed so much in recent years, that it is sometimes not economic to gather the crop.

The nutmeg comes from the Banda Islands in Indonesia and for centuries its source was kept secret because it was such a valuable commodity to the merchants selling it. In 1770 a French naturalist raided the islands, then under Dutch control, and stole several hundred plants and seedlings which were planted on Mauritius and in French Guyana, but these almost all died. At the end of the eighteenth century Britain was at war with Napoleon Bonaparte and Holland, which had allied to France. The British captured the Banda Islands during the war and before they handed them back in 1802 as part of the Treaty of Amiens, they had learnt the secret of the nutmeg and successfully planted it in Penang in Malaya, and tropical territories around the world, including the West Indies, but not Grenada. In 1840 some sugar plantation overseers from Grenada were sent to Penang to help run the newly planted sugar estates there, and they returned home with the first nutmegs to be planted on the island. The first tree is thought to have been planted on the Belvidere Estate in 1843. In 1851 disease swept through the Far Eastern nutmeg plantations, the price rocketed, and Grenadian farmers saw the opportunity, and planted nutmegs in earnest, although it was 30 years later in 1881 before the first were exported.

In 1947 the Grenada Co-operative Nutmeg Association was formed, a farmers' co-operative given the monopoly of all nutmeg exports, and in 1987 agreement was finally reached with Indonesia over managing the world market. Indonesia and Grenada supply virtually all the world's nutmeg, with a 70 per cent and 30 per cent share respectively. That agreement collapsed, however, in 1990 and the Grenadian government had to step in to prevent the collapse of the industry. The industry has

been streamlined where possible, and a distillation plant to extract nutmeg oil is planned which will provide additional income for the producers.

The tree thrives in hilly, wet areas and the fruit is the size of a small tomato. The outer husk, or pericarp, which splits open while still on the tree, is used to make the very popular nutmeg jelly, delicious when spread on toast, desserts or meat.

Inside, the seed is protected by a bright red casing which when dried and crushed, produces the spice mace. Finally, the dark outer shell of the seed is broken open to reveal the nutmeg which is dried and then ground into a powder, or sold whole so that it can be grated to add flavour to dishes.

In Victorian times it was fashionable to carry a nutmeg or wear it in a pendant to ward off illness, and the islanders still use grated nutmeg to help fight colds.

Passion fruit is not widely grown but it can usually be bought at the market. The pulpy fruit contains hundreds of tiny seeds, and many people prefer to press the fruit and drink the juice. It is also

Following pages: Don Philpott and guide at the Dougaldston Estate spice works on Grenada. The guide is holding a cocoa pod

commonly used in fruit salads, sherbets and ice creams.

Pawpaw trees are also found throughout the island and are commonly grown in gardens. The trees are prolific fruit producers but grow so quickly that the fruit soon becomes difficult to gather. The large, juicy melon-like fruits are eaten fresh, pulped for juice or used locally to make jams, preserves and ice cream. They are rich sources of vitamin A and C. The leaves and fruit contain an enzyme which tenderises meat, and tough joints cooked wrapped in pawpaw leaves or covered in slices of fruit, usually taste like much more expensive cuts. The same enzyme, papain, is also used in chewing gum, cosmetics, the tanning industry and, somehow, in making wool shrink resistant. A tea made from unripe fruit is said to be good for lowering high blood pressure.

Pigeon peas are widely cultivated and can be found in many back gardens. The plants are very hardy and drought resistant, and are prolific yields of peas which can be eaten fresh or dried and used in soups and stews.

Pimento, or allspice, was introduced to Grenada from Jamaica. The dried berries are said to have the combined flavours of cinnamon, clove and nutmeg, which is how it gets its name. The dried fruit is used for pickling, for curing meat and flavouring wines, and it is usually an ingredient in curry powder. An oil extracted from the berry and leaf is used in the perfume and pharmaceutical industries.

Pineapples were certainly grown in the Caribbean by the time Columbus arrived, and were probably brought from South America by the Amerindians. The fruit is slightly smaller than the Pacific pineapple, but the flavour more intense.

Sugar cane is grown commercially for making rum. The canes can grow up to 12ft (4m) tall and after cutting, the canes have to be crushed to extract the sugary juice. Most estates had their own sugar mill powered by water wheels or windmills. The remains of many of these mills can still be seen around the island, and much of the original machinery, mostly made in Britain, is still in place. After extraction, the juice is boiled until the sugar crystalises. The mixture remaining is molasses and this is used to produce rum.

Sugar apple is a member of the annona fruit family, and grows wild and in gardens throughout the islands. The small, soft sugar apple fruit can be peeled off in strips when ripe, and is like eating thick apple sauce. They are eaten fresh or used to make sherbet or drinks.

Soursop, is a member of the same family, and its spiny fruits can be seen in hedgerows and gardens. It is eaten fresh or used for preserves, drinks and ice cream.

Turmeric is sold on Grenada as saffron, but it is not. Saffron comes from the dried stigmas of the crocus and is hugely expensive, while turmeric comes from the dried root and underground stems of a plant, which is a relative of ginger. The bright yellow spice is used to flavour foods, and as a colouring. It is also used as a dye.

The **Vanilla plant** is a climbing member of the orchid family which produces long, dangling pods containing beans. The vanilla is extracted by distilling the beans and is used as a food flavouring, as well as in the pharmaceutical industry.

FOOD AND DRINK

Food

Dining out in the Caribbean offers the chance to experiment with all sorts of unusual spices, vegetables and fruits, with creole and island dishes, and, of course, rum punches and other exotic cocktails.

Many hotels have a tendency to offer buffet dinners or barbecues, but even these can be interesting and tasty affairs.

Eating out is generally very relaxed, and few restaurants have a strict dress code, although most people like to wear something a little smarter at dinner after a day on the beach or out sightseeing.

Lunches are best eaten at beach cafés which usually offer excellent barbecued fresh fish and conch — which often appears on menus as lambi (not to be confused with lamb). Lobster and crab are also widely available. Dishes are mostly served with local vegetables such as fried plantain, cassava and yam, and fresh fruit such as pineapple, mango, golden apple or papaya, makes an ideal and light dessert.

There is an enormous choice when it comes to dinner. Starters include traditional Caribbean dishes such as Christophene and coconut soup, and callaloo soup made from the leaves of dasheen, a spinach like vegetable. There is also a strong French tradition with such dishes as soupe Germou made from pumpkin and garlic, and pouile

dudon, a chicken stew with coconut and molasses. Fish and clam chowders are also popular starters. Try heart of palm, excellent fresh shrimps or scallops, smoked kingfish wrapped in crepes or crab backs, succulent land crab meat sauteed with breadcrumbs and seasoning, and served restuffed in the shell. It is much sweeter than the meat of sea crabs.

The fish is generally excellent, and do not be alarmed if you see dolphin on the menu. It is not the protected species made famous by 'Flipper', but a solid, close-textured flat faced fish called dorado, which is delicious. There is also snapper, tuna, lobster, swordfish, baby squid and mussels.

Try seafood jambalaya, chunks of lobster, shrimps and ham served on a bed of braised seasoned rice, shrimp creole, with fresh shrimp sauted in garlic butter and parsley and served with tomatoes, or fish creole, with fresh fish steaks cooked in a spicy onion, garlic and tomato sauce and served with rice and fried plaintain. Other island specialities include sauted scallops with ginger, curried fish steaks lightly fried with a curry sauce and served with sliced bananas, cucumber, fresh coconut and rice.

It seems such a waste to travel to the Caribbean and eat burgers and steaks, especially when there are many much more exciting meat dishes available.

You could try curried chicken served in a coconut shell, curried goat, gingered chicken with mango and spices, or Caribbean souse, with cuts of lean pork marinated with shredded cucumber, onions, garlic, lime juice and pepper sauce.

For vegetarians there are excellent salads, stuffed breadfruit, callaloo bake, stuffed squash and pawpaw, baked sweet potato and yam casserole.

For dessert, try fresh fruit salad, or one of the exotically flavoured ice creams. There are also banana fritters and banana flambe, coconut cheesecake and tropical fruit sorbets.

Most menus and dishes are self explanatory, but one or two things are worth bearing in mind. When green fig appears on the menu, it usually means green banana, which is peeled and boiled as a vegetable.

On the buffet table, you will

Preceding pages: St George's as viewed from the south

often see a dish called pepper pot. This is usually a hot, spicy meat and vegetable stew to which may be added small flour dumplings and shrimps.

There are wonderful breads in the Caribbean, and you should try them if you get the chance. There are banana and pumpkin breads, and delicious cakes such as coconut loaf cake, guava jelly cookies and rum cake.

Do not be afraid to eat out. Food is often prepared in front of you, and there are some great snacks available from island eateries. Try deep fried cakes of dough called floats, or saltfish or corned beef fritters, or coconut patties.

You must try roti, an East Indian creation, which is available almost everywhere. It is a paper thin dough wrapped round a spicy, hot curry mixture, and contains beef, chicken, vegetables or fish. The chicken roti often contains bones which some people like to chew on, so be warned.

Drink

Rum is the Caribbean drink. There are almost as many rums in the West Indies as their are malt whiskies in Scotland (Britain), and there is an amazing variety of strength, colour and quality. The finest rums are best drunk on the rocks, but if you want to capture a bit of the Caribbean spirit, have a couple of rum punches. Carriacou produces the very strong Jack Iron rum, or 'Jack'.

To make Plantation Rum Punch, thoroughly mix 3 ounces of rum, with 1 ounce of lime juice and 1 teaspoon of honey, then pour over crushed ice, and add a pinch of freshly grated nutmeg.

Most hotels and bars also offer a wide range of cocktails both alcoholic, usually very strong, and non-alcoholic. Beer, drunk cold and from the bottle, is the most popular drink, and wine, where available, is often expensive because of taxes, and the choice limited.

Tap water is safe to drink as are ice cubes made from it. Mineral and bottled water is widely available, as are soft drinks.

NOTE

While many of the restaurants do offer excellent service, time does not always have the same urgency as it does back home, and why should it? After all, as you are on holiday, relax, enjoy a drink, the company and the surroundings and do not worry if things take just a little longer. The wait is generally worth it.

Touring & Exploring Grenada

Grenada consists of six parishes, St. George and St. David in the south, St. Andrew along the east coast, St. Patrick in the north, St. Mark, the smallest in the north-west, and St. John on the west coast. The island is easy to explore with roads running around the entire coastline and others traversing the island or providing access to remote inland areas. Most roads are paved although care needs to be taken especially in the countryside because of pot holes and other hazards. Many of the roads are not very wide and care is needed when passing, especially as there are often very sharp corners, and in places no hard shoulders and steep drops. Landslides are also quite common after very heavy rains.

The Carenage from Fort George, St George's

GETTING AROUND GRENADA

Taxis: Plentiful, fun and cheap. The drivers are knowledgeable and make good guides, and if you do not want to drive yourself, you can hire taxis by the hour or day. There are fixed fares on main routes ie EC$30 from St. George's to the airport, and EC$7 for journeys of 1 mile (2km) or less. Longer journeys generally cost EC$4 1 mile (2km) for the first 10 miles (16km), then EC$3 1 mile (2km) after that. There is a EC$10 surcharge after 6pm. If hiring the taxi for a tour, always negotiate the price of the journey before setting off, and make sure you both know which currency (EC$ or US$) you are going to pay in.

Water taxis: Available from the Carenage St. George's. You can catch a water taxi to get to other points on the Carenage, the cruise pier and Grand Anse. Taxis and mini buses for hire have registration numbers beginning with the letter 'H'.

Mini-buses: The fun way to get around provided you check that the bus is heading in your direction, and that there is one back. You can catch buses from most destinations in Market Square or along the Esplanade. There are fixed fares from EC$1.25 to EC$5 according to the distance travelled. There are few buses after dark or on Sundays. From St. George's expect to pay EC$1 to Grand Anse, EC$2 to Concorde, EC$3 to Grand Etang, EC$4.50 to Genville, and EC$5 to sauteurs.

Horse and carriage: Tour St. George's and area in style in a traditional horse and carriage.

Hire cars: Cars, four-wheel drive vehicles, scooters and bicycles can all be hired.

Air: Helenair Grenada is available for day tour charters, aerial photography, air ambulance and transfers for international connections. ☎ 444-2266. Arlines of Carriacou have daily scheduled flights to Carriacou, Union Island, Bequia and St. Vincent.

ST. GEORGE'S

Many people consider St. George's, Grenada's capital, as the most picturesque city in the Caribbean, nestling as it does on the hillsides that slope down to the water's edge. Historic forts still 'guard' the city, and houses with their lush gardens, cling precariously to the hillsides. In the heart of the city there are cobbled streets to explore, markets to visit, eateries to enjoy and a wealth of history to absorb.

St. George's is really split in two by a hill which runs from Fort George inland, and separates the Carenage and harbour area from the area known as Bay Town, which makes up the western side of the city. The two areas are connected by the Sendall Tunnel, opened in 1895 and named after Governor Sir Walter Sendall. It is 340ft (104m) long and 12ft (3m) high, and when built was a major engineering feat.

The horseshoe-shaped Carenage is the heart of the city and runs round the inner harbour. The tourist office is sited in a new building on the waterfront, and makes a great place to start your walking tour of the city.

On foot is the best way of getting around St. George's because many of the streets are very narrow. There are many blind corners, which is why there are police traffic controls, and traffic can be chaotic at peak periods. It is much better if you have a hire car, to leave it safely parked, and to set out and explore on foot.

You will quickly get used to the noise and the atmosphere. Grenadians toot their horns whenever they see someone they know, and as everyone seems to know everyone else, drivers spend almost all their time tooting to say hello, or tooting back in reply. If you can ignore the tooting, you will not be able to ignore the radios and stereo systems which are usually played at maximum volume.

When you pass one of the often seen lines of immaculately dressed children, hand in hand, and wearing school uniforms and smiles from ear to ear, wave and smile back. On Grenada, everyone is happy.

The Carenage gets its name because in the old days, ships were hauled up on to the beach here and laid on their sides, or 'careened' so that repairs could be carried out and barnacles scraped off the hull.

For centuries the harbour has been the heart of the city. St. George's owes its growth to its deep, natural harbour, the remnants of a submerged volcanic crater. The sheltered anchorage, protected on most sides by hills, was strategically important and over the centuries was fought over by the British and French. Altogether six forts were built by the French and British to protect it and the sea approaches. Three of the forts remain: Fort George, built by the French between 1706 and 1710 to protect the harbour and the surrounding seas, and Fort Matthew and Fort Frederick on Richmond Hill which have fabulous views over the city, harbour, surrounding countryside and sea beyond. Forts Adolphus and Lucas have not survived, nor has the original French stockade built in 1650.

From this vantage point, you can look over the city and see just

how sprawling it has become, although this in no way detracts from its charm. From the fort you can also see just how much greenery there is, with carefully tended gardens, palms and lush vegetation.

The original town was around the waterfront and many of the streets are steep, narrow and cobbled, and full of fascinating shops and kiosks. There are red telephone kiosks and pillar boxes, and old cannons have been upended and stuck in the road to act as bollards.

From the Carenage you can look out over the harbour to the cruise ship berth to the left, and Fort George, standing proudly on the hill overlooking the entrance to the harbour on the right. The harbour itself is usually busy with fishing boats and charter ships. The view at night with the twinkling lights is just as enchanting.

The 800ft (244m) pier has berths for two or three ocean going vessels up to 500ft (152m) long, as well as cargo vessels, and there is a 250ft (76m) long schooner pier. The port also has container port, warehouses and bonded storage facilities. There is usually at least one majestic cruise ship visiting, with others anchored offshore. The entrance to the harbour is

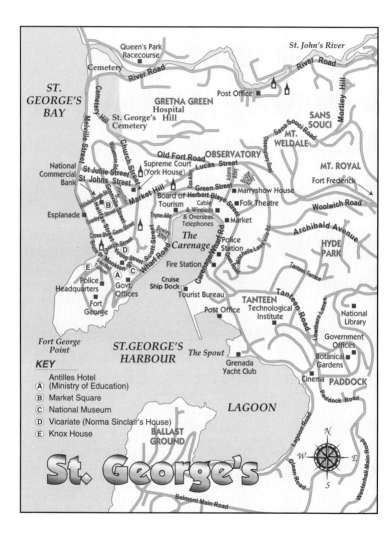

Queen's Park
Racecourse
St. John's River
Cemetery
River Road
River Road
Mortley Hill
ST. GEORGE'S BAY
Post Office
GRETNA GREEN
Hospital
St. George's Hill
Cemetery
SANS SOUCI
Sans Souci Road
MT. WELDALE
Melville Street
Cemetery Hill
Church Street
Old Fort Road
OBSERVATORY
Supreme Court
(York House)
Lucas Street
Adams Alley
MT. ROYAL
Fort Frederick
National Commercial Bank
St Julile Street
St Johns Street
Market Hill
Green Street
Board of Tourism
Herbert Blaze St
Cable & Wireless & Overseas Telephones
Marryshow House
Folk Theatre
Woolwich Road
Esplanade
Hillsborough Street
Granby Street
Grenville Street
Cross Street Gore Street
Tyne Alle
Bowley Alley
Market
Archibald Avenue
HYDE PARK
The Carenage
Police Station
Carenage Wharf Rd
Mitchells Lane
Lagoon Road
Church Street
Young Street
Scott Street
Wharf Road
Fire Station
Tanteen Terrace
Police Headquarters
Govt Offices
Cruise Ship Dock
Tourist Bureau
Post Office
TANTEEN
Technological Institute
Tanteen Road
Lowthers Lanes
National Library
Fort George
Fort George Point
ST. GEORGE'S HARBOUR
The Spout
Grenada Yacht Club
Government Offices
Botanical Gardens
Cinema
PADDOCK
Paddock Road

KEY
(A) Antilles Hotel (Ministry of Education)
(B) Market Square
(C) National Museum
(D) Vicariate (Norma Sinclair's House)
(E) Knox House

LAGOON

BALLAST GROUND

St. George's

Lagoon Road
Glean Road
Westerhall Main Road

N
W E
S

Belmont Main Road

protected by buoys and is 600ft (183m) wide and 45ft (14m) deep.

There are a number of eating places along the Carenage, as well as tourist shops and outdoor stalls selling souvenirs, handicrafts and paintings by local artists. The offices of Grentel are about 900ft (274m) north-west of the tourist information centre.

A number of water-taxis operate from the **Carenage** and will ferry you to other points along the waterfront, or to further afield destinations such as Grand Anse beach. There are also larger vessels offering day time and dinner cruises, such as the *Treasure Queen* and two *Rhum Runners*, noted for their rum punches and music. As a reminder of the island's recent troubles, you can see the burnt out hull of a ship protruding from the harbour, a victim of the 1983 intervention.

Walk along the Carenage past the Ristorante Italia and Sand Pebbles Restaurants, and follow the harbour, past The Nutmeg, another eatery, to the junction of the Carenage and Young Street. Notice the cobblestones and the ways the cannons have been used for traffic control. Continue along the Carenage, past Rudolf's

Restaurant to Matthew Street with the **National Library** on the corner. The library was established in 1846 and has been housed in this former brick warehouse since 1892. The **Post Office** is further along the Carenage, having been moved from its old site after a fire in 1990, but take Matthew Street to visit the **Antilles Hotel** and the National Museum, close to its junction with Young Street. The Antilles Hotel is one of the oldest buildings in St. George's. It started out as a French barracks, then became a British prison, then a hotel and then a warehouse. There are hopes that it might become a hotel again. It is now generally known as the building housing the Ministry of Education.

The small **National Museum**, built on the foundations of a former French army barracks and prison built in 1704 (it still has some dungeons) has a fine collection of exhibits tracing the island's history and culture, with Arawak and Carib artefacts. It is open Monday to Friday 9am-4.30pm, Saturday 10am-4pm.

Turn left into Young Street and then right into Church Street. At the top of Young Street a smartly uniformed police officer directs the hectic traffic during the day.

Church Street runs along the hill

dividing the Carenage area and the Bay Town areas. It gets its name because along its length are the **Roman Catholic Cathedral** with its 1818 tower, the St. George's **Anglican Church**, rebuilt in Georgian style in 1826, on the site of a building built by French Catholics, and the **St. Andrew's Presbyterian Church** and **Knox House**, before the climb up to Fort George. The Anglican Church, built in 1825, is noted for its stone and pink stucco, and has a number of interesting plaques and statues, and the Presbyterian Church, built between 1830 and 1831, also known as the Scots Kirk, was built with the help of the Freemasons.

Just beyond St. Andrew's, Church Street runs over the Sendall Tunnel road which connects the Carenage and Bay Town areas of the city.

Fort George is a bastioned fort built by the French. It was later taken over by the British and extended. The original fort, however, was a wooden stockade built by the French in 1650 and had two cannon to protect the original settlement of Port Louis. The stone fort was built in 1706 to protect the new town when Port Louis was abandoned and Port Royale established, and was known as Fort Royale until the British gave it its present name. It is the oldest structure on the island, and while it commanded the sea approaches to the town, it was vulnerable because it was overlooked by higher ground to the north. So, over the next few years, additional fortifications were added to try to rectify this.

Today the fort offers spectacular views in all directions, and you can explore the tunnels and interior, and walk along the battlements with its many cannons. The Grenada National Trust and Historical Society, with funding from USAID, are refurbishing the fort and lighting. Some exhibits and interpretive signs have already been installed.

The fort was built as the first in a series protecting the harbour, town and coastline, the others being the batteries at Butler Hill to the south, formerly the Monckton Hill redoubt, and Moliniere Point to the north. The fort did not see action until late in the eighteenth century, when on 4 July 1779 the French with 10,000 troops, invaded Grenada and the town was captured. The British were taken completely by surprise because the French troops had been landed a few miles along the coast and they marched inland in order to attack St.

George's from its unprotected flank. The fortifications specially built to protect Fort George, were all designed to repel an attack from the sea, and there were no defences against a landward attack. The British surrendered, and the French realising the vulnerability of the defences, immediately started work on a ring of forts to protect the town from attack from inland.

Fort George was the scene of Grenada's assumption of independence on 7 February 1974, and on 13 March 1979, it was the last symbol of authority of the regime overthrown by the New Jewel Movement, who renamed it Fort Rubert. The fort was also the centre of the island's political turmoil, when on 19 October 1983 Maurice Bishop and ten members of his cabinet were executed by a faction of the People's Revolutionary Government. It is now the headquarters of the Royal Grenada Police Force and has barracks and the training school for new recruits, although it is open to the public. Near the crest of the hill is the hospital in what used to be the fort's military barracks.

From the vantage point of the fort, you can look over the city and just below you, between the fort and the harbour, you can see the historic, red-tiled roofed, brick eighteenth- and nineteenth-century warehouses. The tiles were brought to the islands as ballast in European trading ships.

Retrace your steps back along Church Street past the Scots Kirk, and then turn left for about 100ft (30m) and then left again into Cross Street which leads to the Esplanade. Enjoy the walk along the Esplanade, then turn right into Hillsborough Street for Market Square, bordered by Hillsborough, Halifax, Granby and Grenville Streets.

The Bay Town area is dominated by the **Market Square**, which is an entertainment ❈ in its own right. It is a blaze of colourful umbrella-shaded stalls bearing fruits, vegetables, spices and herbs of all descriptions, as well as handicrafts such as woven baskets, bamboo brooms and straw hats and bags. There are more stalls inside the tin roofed market buildings.

It is a typical market, full of noise and activity and not just a place for buying and selling, but a gathering place for people from around the island. You can get a refreshing drink of coconut 'milk', drunk straight from a freshly-opened nut, and try some of the island delicacies such as a salt fish sandwich, or slices of fried black

GRENADA

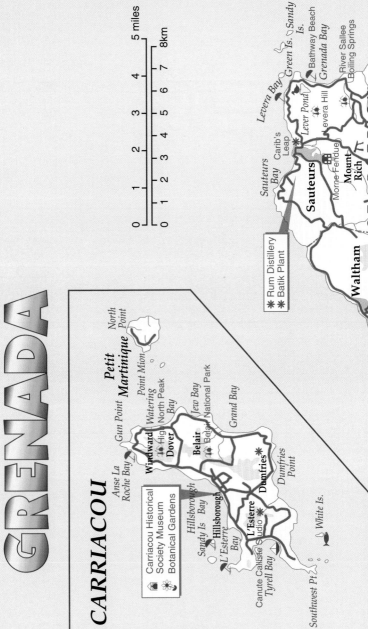

CARRIACOU

Anse La Roche Bay

Gun Point · North Point

Petit Martinique

Point Mion

Windward · Watering Bay

High North Peak

Dover · New Bay

Belair · Belair National Park

Grand Bay

Dumfries · Dumfries Point

Carriacou Historical Society Museum · Botanical Gardens

Hillsborough · Hillsborough Bay

Sandy Is · Bay

L'Esterre · L'Esterre Bay · L'Esterre Studio

Canute Calliste Studio · Tyrell Bay

Southwest Pt. · White Is.

0 1 2 3 4 5 miles
0 1 2 3 4 5 6 7 8km

Levera Bay · Green Is. · Sandy Is.

Bathway Beach · Grenada Bay

River Sallee Boiling Springs

Lever Pond · Levera Hill

Sauteurs Bay · Carib's Leap

Sauteurs

Morne Fendue

Mount Rich

ST PATRICK

Waltham

Victoria

Antoine

* Rum Distillery
✳ Batik Plant

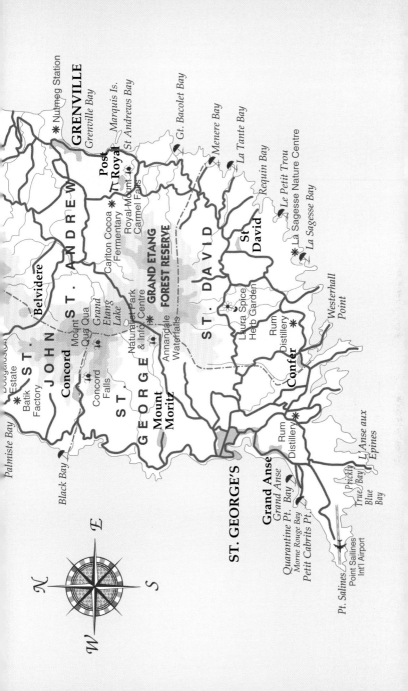

pudding. It is also a great place for buying many of the special products made from the island's spices, such as jellies, jams and sauces.

The Market Square was opened in 1791 and has always played a prominent role in the island's history. It was the site of the early slave market, and the scene for public executions. After the unsuccessful Fedon Rebellion of 1795-6, the captured rebels were hanged in the square. A section of the square also serves as the main bus station, but always make sure you know where the mini bus is going before boarding, and shop around, because you may get a better price from another driver. The square is used for political meetings and rallies.

✳ **Bay Town** now called **"Esplanade"** used to be a quiet residential area overlooking the city, with delightful, tree-shaded walks and beaches, and noted for its water fountain. Today, it has been overtaken by the city, and the Esplanade, which runs alongside the western shoreline, is also a picking up and dropping off for mini buses which ply around the island. There is now a medical centre here, as well as a number of small shops and eateries. Surrounding streets have

interesting shops and bazaars, and do not be surprised to see chickens and tethered goats.

After exploring the market and buying provisions and souvenirs, turn right again on Grenville Street and then right into St. Juille Street which meets Church Street. To your left is the old **Vicariate** of the Roman Catholic Cathedral which is just down on your right. The Vicariate, also referred to as **Norma Sinclair's House** was built between 1914 and 1918 and given to the Presentation Brothers in 1947 for a college. The cathedral's tower dates from 1818, although the present church was built in 1884 on the site of the original 1804 building. Follow Church Street south to take in the Houses of Parliament. **York House**, named after the Duke of York's visit to the island in the eighteenth century, was purchased in 1801 and is home of the House of Representatives, the Senate and the Supreme Court. York House and the neighbouring Registry, built in 1780, are fine examples of early Georgian architecture. Then note the buildings on your right with their sedan porches. The porches used to be opened at both ends so that passengers in sedan chairs could get out in the dry when it was raining.

Then continue down Church Street for St. George's Anglican Church. You can take Simmons Alley which curves round the church, and then the steps

leading to Scott Street. Head north along Scott Street, that is away from the sea, to the police traffic control point at the end, and then cross over into Lucas Street which takes you to Richmond Hill and Fort Frederick.

Fort Frederick was completed in 1791 and is also a bastion-type fort. It had the largest guns on the island, capable of firing 32lb (14kgm) shots. Towards the end of the nineteenth century, the fort's huge underground cisterns were utilised by the city to provide a water supply. It was the headquarters of the People's Revolutionary Army during the 1983 intervention, and saw action, the scars of which can still be seen. The fortifications have now largely been restored, and the views from the battlements are well worth the walk.

Although it is not open to the public, you can view **Fort Matthew** from Fort Frederick. It is a classic siege fort built by the French in 1779. Its huge walls and nine massively protected gun chambers were designed to withstand any attack, and there were a further sixteen gun

positions — all facing inland. The extensive fort had barracks for soliders, officers, as well as married quarters, two huge water cisterns for storing more than 80,000 gallons of water, cobbler's shop, parade ground and kitchen garden. There was also a series of tunnels so that soldiers could move safely between barracks and gun emplacements if under attack. The whole structure was further protected by a deep dry moat. It has been suggested that all the forts protecting the city were connected by tunnels, and although many tunnels have been found, most were bricked off so it is not known where they led. In 1854 when the British withdrew their forces from the Caribbean, Fort Matthew became the Windward Island's first mental asylum, and it was used as such until it was accidentally bombed in 1983 and finally abandoned in 1987. For several years it was derelict, but in 1989 it was adopted by the Grenada National Trust and restoration plans are now well under way. The eighteenth-century kitchen, in use until 1987, has been cleaned and the plaster removed, revealing the original arched brick ceiling. The central courtyard and some tunnels have also been cleared.

From Fort Frederick you can also

FORT WILLIAM

Fort William used to stand at Old Fort, 500ft (152m) above sea level and protecting the northern end of St. George's, and able to cover Fort George if it was attacked. Its huge, long range guns could hit targets a long way out to sea, and anything that escaped this barrage and attempted to sail closer, would have come within range of the batteries at Fort George. Fort William was built by the French in 1738, and was again one of three major defences constructed to protect the northern flanks of the town. The powder chamber and a small prison were actually dug out of the hillside. When a French force led by D'Estaing landed on Grenada in 1779, Fort William was the first defensive position to be attacked. Rather than risk a frontal attack on the town protected by Fort George, the French landed up the coast and made their way inland so they could make a surprise attack on Fort William. The English were routed and on 4 July the town and Fort George surrendered.

The French realised how vulnerable the forts were if attacked from inland, and immediately set about building even more fortifications. Although Grenada was ceded to the English by the Treaty of Versailles in 1783, work on the forts was completed and by 1791 four new forts had been built — Matthew and Frederick, and the two smaller forts Lucas and Adolfus.

look down to the island's prison, formerly for the fort's hospital, with its neat vegetable gardens tended by the inmates.

Retrace your way down Lucas Street and then take the steps leading down to Green Street. Turn right past the St. George's **Methodist Church**, built in 1820, and the oldest original church building in the city, and then turn sharp left into Herbert Blaye Street (formerly Tyrrel Street and renamed in honour of the former Prime Minister) to visit **Marryshow House** which is on the corner of Herbert Blaye Street and Park Lane. It was the former home of T.A. Marryshow, who campaigned for one West Indian

Facing page: Boats in the Carenage at St George's

nation, and is known as the 'Father of the Federation'. It is now the local centre for the University of the West Indies. The Maryshow Folk Theatre stages a programme of concerts and plays. Further up the hill, above Marryshow House is **Government House**, built in 1802 and set in its own grounds behind large iron gates. Retrace your steps along Herbert Blaye Street for about 300ft (91m), before turning left for the short walk back to the Carenage and the tourist office.

There is a 9 hole golf course close to St. George's off the appropriately named Golf Course Street. There are also plenty of facilities for tennis, and land and water-based sports. Many of these facilities are provided by the hotels and resorts, but are usually open to non-guests.

January is a busy time in and around St. George's with major events including the Billfishing Tournament, which attracts an international field of top anglers, the International Triathlon open to both men and women, and Grenada's annual Sailing Festival, which also attracts yachts from around the world.

Independence Day is 7 February, and the event is celebrated throughout the island with church services and a parade in Queen's Park. The biggest event of the year, however, is Carnival, held on the second weekend of August. A Carnival Queen is chosen, and there are competitions to find the best steelband, calypso, costumed band and so on. It is a hectic and fun-filled 5 days of dancing and partying from Friday to Tuesday.

Other places to visit include: **St. George's Cemetery**, on the western outskirts of town on Old Fort Road, with its old and interesting graves; the **Botanical Gardens**, opened in 1887 and a 5 minute drive east out of St. George's, with displays of many of the island's native plants and flowers; and **Bay Garden**, in the suburb of St. Paul's, which has meandering paths through the several acres of fine tropical gardens with exotic trees, flowers and shrubs. There is a small admission fee but it is worth it for the conducted tour which provides an insight into the island's main crops and spices. Also in St. Paul's, is **de La Grenade Industries**, a spice processing plant which has won international awards for its nutmeg products such as jams, jellies and syrups, and liqueurs made from local fruits and spices. It is open to visitors and tours are offered. Just north of the city is **Queen's**

Park, the venue for all major sporting events, as well as parades and concerts.

The **Annandale Falls** are a 15 minute drive north-east of St. George's on the way to Grand Etang, and worth visiting because of their location rather than the size of the cascade. The 30ft (9m) falls, surrounded by dasheen and vines, are in the hills south of Grand Etang Lake and surrounded by lush, tropical vegetation. The water flow drops substantially in the dry season, but the pool below the falls is inviting and there is a rest room with changing and washing facilities.

For a full day out with a picnic, consider a trip to the **Seven Sisters Waterfalls**, which are high in the Eastern Mountains in dense vegetation and at the end of a difficult 1 hour's walk from the road. The falls are on private land and there is an admission charge, and a guide for this trip is essential. The Royal Mount Carmel Waterfalls offer a much more convenient option; see page 86 for further details.

EATING OUT

In and Around St. George's

Inexpensive	$
Moderate	$$
Expensive	$$$

Bobby's Health Stop $-$$
On Gore Street, St. George's and in the Le Marquis complex, food for the health conscious (☎ 440-7080)

Chef's Castle $
Gore and Halifax Street, St. George's, fast food (☎ 440-4778)

De Water Hole $
Opposite the Botanic Gardens, St. George's, local snacks and ice cream

Deyna's $-$$
Melville Street, St. George's, West Indian (☎ 440-6795)

Green Flash Restaurant $$-$$$
Overlooks St. George's, International/Middle Eastern (☎ 444-4645)

Hole in the Wall $$
Carenage, West Indian (☎ 440-3158)

Judith's $$
Gore Street, St. George's, West Indian (☎ 440-5732)

Kentucky Fried Chicken $
Granby Street, St. George's, fast food (☎ 440-3821)

Kwality Restaurant $-$$
Corner of Cross and Melville Streets, St. George's, West Indian and East Indian (☎ 440-5206)

BIANCA C

The luxury cruise liner *Bianca C* sank off Point Salines in 1961 and she is by far the largest of the wrecks that are scattered off Grenada's shores. The 600ft (183m) long, 18,000 ton cruise ship was a frequent visitor to Grenada and was often seen anchored in St. George's outer harbour. On 22 October 1961, however, residents were aware that something was wrong because the ship was repeatedly sounding her fog horn. The ship was on fire and needed urgent help. A huge explosion had ripped through the engine room and the fire was fast spreading through the ship. Every boat in the harbour was manned, including rowing boats, and a race against time started to rescue the 400 passengers and 300 crew on board. As explosions ripped through the ship, all the passengers and most of the crew were safely rescued. Finally, the Captain and the officers that had remained on board with him were taken off. The rescue, which took 2 hours to complete, then led to another major problem. Almost 700 survivors needed to be fed, clothed and accommodated and the whole island lent a helping hand.

The following day, the ship was still on fire and in danger of sinking and blocking the harbour. The frigate *HMS Londonderry* was sent for, and before dawn the next day, a line had been put on board and the burning ship was slowly towed out of harbour. The plan had been to try to beach the ship on a reef close to the southern tip of the island, but strong winds swung the *Bianca C* round, the towing cable broke, and she started to sink almost immediately. The survivors spent a further week as the islander's guests before two ships arrived to take them away. Grenadian W.E. Julian, who represented the Costa Steamship Line, owners of the cruise ship, and largely co-ordinated the repatriation of the passengers and crew, was made a Cavalier of the Order of Merit by the Italian government, and the steamship company presented the people of Grenada with a life size bronze replica of the statue *Christ of the Deep*. Despite a bitter row over who should pay for siting the statue, it was erected by the council on the eastern arm of the harbour. It has since been moved and now stands on the Carenage at the head of the harbour. The plaque reads: 'To the people of Grenada in grateful remembrance of the fraternal Christian hospitality shown to passengers and crew of the Italian liner *Bianca C* destroyed by fire in this harbor on October 22, 1961. Dedicated by the Costa Line of Genoa, Italy.'

A Grenadian nutmeg works

Le Bistro $$-$$$
Ross Point, French/West Indian
(☎ 444-0191)

Little Bakery Coffee House $-$$
Grand Anse Street, St. George's
West Indian (☎ 444-3623)

Mamma's $$
Near Grenada Yacht Club, West
Indian (☎ 440-1459) reservations
preferred

Nutmeg $-$$
Carenage, above the Sea Change
Book Shop, West Indian/
international (☎ 440-2539)

Portofino Ristorante Italia $$

Carenage, Italian (☎ 440-3986)

Rudolf's $$-$$$
Carenage, Continental/West
Indian/seafood (☎ 440-2241)

Sand Pebbles $-$$
Carenage, West Indian/snacks
(☎ 440-2688)

Traffic Light Bar & Grill $-$$
Belmont, St. George's, West
Indian (☎ 440-3375)

Tropicana $-$$
Lagoon Road, St. George's,
Chinese/West Indian (☎ 440-
1586)

SOUTH OF ST. GEORGE'S & THE SOUTH COAST

St. George's is in the parish of St. George which has a population of around 32,000, and covers the south-western corner of the island, including the splendid Grand Anse Bay, the main resort area with its world famous, sandy beaches. As with the entire coastal drive, there are fabulous views round almost every turn, as well as great sweeping vistas from vantage points over sandy, near deserted beaches and warm, inviting seas.

Travelling south out of St.

George's one follows the coast road past the Grenada Yacht Club which sits on a promontory overlooking the lagoon and back to the Carenage. The lagoon is a popular anchorage for yachts.

Grand Anse Bay has a spectacular 2 mile (3km) long beach of white sand and warm, clear waters. A coral reef at the mouth of the bay makes it ideal for safe swimming and snorkelling.

Grand Anse is the island's main resort area with many large

hotels, holiday cottages and apartments, and a number of fine restaurants and shopping complexes. There are plans to establish a vendor's market at one end of the beach and then ban selling elsewhere on the beach so that tourists are not pestered. The Old Sugar Mill Factory has now been converted into a night club.

The road then continues south past **Quarantine Point**, named because British troops who got smallpox were hospitalised here in the nineteenth century, to the south-western tip of the island and Point Salines and the international airport. The stretch of coastline between Petits Cabrits Point and Point Salines has some fabulous beaches, and the waters are great for diving. You can also visit the Portici ruins by the beach. **Point Salines** lighthouse stands at the tip of the headland, the most westerly point on Grenada. From the point you can look south to Glover Island, which was a Norwegian run whaling station early in the twentieth century.

There are a number of very pretty bays and headlands along this stretch of coastline, and there are some fine houses with magnificent views. Much of this area around the airport used to be devoted to sugar cane and sheep rearing, but a lot of the land has

been sold for residential development, and there are even more expensive beach-side homes.

Yachts can dock at jetties in **True Blue Bay** and neighbouring Prickly Bay, and there are two marinas at L'Anse aux Epines, offering services to both visiting yachts, and holidaymakers wanting to charter vessels for a day cruise or longer.

Calivigny Point was the site of the People's Revolutionary Army's main camp and saw a lot of military action when US troops came ashore, and Fort Jeudy used to guard the entrance to Egmont Harbour, although it has long since disappeared, and the area is now occupied by expensive homes.

The **parish of St. David** covers the south-eastern corner of the island and has a population of around 11,000. It is the only parish on the island without a town of any size, although there are many villages in this predominantly agricultural area producing mainly sugar cane, cocoa, bananas, nutmeg and other spices.

This area has a beautiful stretch of coastline with scores of small bays and inlets, where you can really get away from the crowds, and find a small, sandy beach all for yourself.

Yachts can jetty at True Blue Bay

The area around the boundaries of the parishes of St. George and St. David, is one of the few remaining habitats of the rare Grenada Dove, and reserves have been established to protect it.

Shortly after crossing into the parish of St. David, on the Southern Main Road, you will see the entrance of the **Westerhall Estate**, most famous for its rum distillery which has been distilling rum in the traditional way since 1800. The estate formerly produced sugar cane and the massive old iron water wheel which used to crush the cane can still be seen although it no longer operates. About 100 years ago, the nearby river was diverted to run by the factory to drive the wheel which turned the machinery which extracted the juice from the cane to make the

Facing page: Grand Anse Bay, with one of the islands best beaches

rum. The estate no longer crushes its own cane, but buys in molasses for the distillation.

Westerhall produces a number of different rums from the very smooth Westerhall Plantation Rum to Jack Iron, aged in oak barrels, and Wester-all Strong Rum, best sipped on its own to appreciate its full flavour and aroma.

Between Confer and the distillery, a road runs off on the right to **Westerhall Point**, once part of the estate, and now a private development with a number of fine homes, many with their own private beach fronts.

Continuing along the coast, you can visit the **La Sagesse Nature Centre**. The centre occupies a house built by the late Lord Brownlow, who was equerry to the Duke of Windsor when he abdicated from the British throne in 1936 to marry the American divorcee Mrs Simpson. The house and estate was bought by the Government in 1970. There is a restaurant by the white sandy **La Sagesse beach** and the opportunity for a dip, although the water is very shallow for quite a way out to sea. This area was one of the first settled in Grenada, although there are no signs of the original colony which was known as Megrin. It is possible to arrange hikes and nature walks into the woods and mangrove estuary which teems with bird life.

The rest of the estate has been divided into 5 acre (2 hectare) agricultural lots which are worked by experienced farmers as part of a Government-backed model farm experiment. Both the French Government and Republic of China are cooperating on schemes to improve irrigation systems, and to introduce new plants and crops.

Off La Sagesse Point lies the wreck of the *SS Orinoco*, which foundered on the rocks on All Saints Day, 1 November 1900. It was the custom at that time on All Saints Day to light a candle on the graves of loved ones. The ship's captain mistakenly thought the many lights were the lights of St. George's so turned towards them and hit the rocks.

From Content village, there is a short walk down to the charming **Le Petit Trou beach**. The road then continues uphill to **St. David's** where there is a small police station and post office. A little further along, there is a small road off on the right leading down to **Requin Bay**, which used to be a flourishing little port shipping out cocoa and nutmeg. Much of the materials for the small Catholic church on the cliffs was brought in by ships docking there. While inland, near **Perdmontemps**, you can visit the Laura Spice and Herb Garden (both open daily), which displays the island's spices grown in their natural habitat.

EATING OUT

In Grand Anse/Morne Rouge

Inexpensive	$
Moderate	$$
Expensive	$$$

Bad Ass Cafe $$
Le Marquis Complex, Mexican (☎ 444-4020)

Beach Side Terrace Restaurant $$-$$$
Flamboyant Hotel, Grand Anse, West Indian/Continental (☎ 444-4247). Fabulous views day and night.

Bird's Nest $-$$
Grand Anse, Chinese/Creole (☎ 444-4264)

Camerhogne Park Restaurant $-$$
Morne Rouge, Grenadian/Continental (☎ 444-4587)

Canboulay $$
Grand Anse, West Indian/International (☎ 444-4401)

Coconut's Beach $$-$$$
Grand Anse Beach, French Creole (☎ 444-4644)

Cot Bam $-$$
Grand Anse, West Indian (☎ 444-2050)

Coyaba $$-$$$
Grand Anse Beach, West Indian/International (☎ 444-4129)

Fish & Chick $-$$
Old Sugar Mill, Grand Anse, fast food (☎ 444-4132)

Green Flash Restaurant $$
Siesta Hotel, West Indian/International (☎ 444-4645)

Grenada Renaissance Terrace $$-$$$
Grand Anse, Creole/International (☎ 444-4371)

Hibiscus Hotel $$
Morne Rouge, Continental/Creole (☎ 444-4008)

Jade Garden $$
Mace Hotel, Morne Rouge, Chinese (☎ 444-3698)

Joe's Steakhouse $$
Le Marquis Centre, steaks and fish (☎ 444-4020)

Following pages: Coconuts are extensively grown on the island but can be a hazard!

La Belle Creole $$-$$$
Blue Horizons Cottage Hotel,
Morne Rouge, West Indian/
Continental (☎ 444-4316)

La Dolce Vita $$
Cinnamon Hill Hotel, Grand Anse,
Italian (☎ 444-4301)

La Sagesse Nature Centre $-$$
La Sagesse Beach, Continental/
seafood (☎ 444-6458)

Liftoff $-$$$
Point Salines Airport, West Indian/
International (☎ 444-4101)

Nick's Donut World $
Grand Anse, donuts and ice
cream (☎ 444-2460)

Parrots Cafe & Bar $
Grand Anse, Mexican
(☎ 444-5083)

Rick's Cafe $
Grand Anse Shopping Plaza, fast
food (☎ 444-4597)

Roydon's $$
Roydon's Guest House, Grand
Anse, Continental/West Indian
(☎ 444-4476)

South Winds $$-$$$
Grand Anse above South Winds
Cottages, West Indian/International
(☎ 444-4310)

Spice Island Inn $$-$$$
Grand Anse, West Indian/
International (☎ 444-4258)

**Sur La Mer Restaurant and
Aquarius Beach Pavilion** $$-$$$
Gem Holiday Resort, Morne Rouge,
West Indian/International/seafood
(☎ 444-4224)

Tabanca at Journey's End $-$$
Grand Anse, cafe/bistro
(☎ 444-1300)

Windward Sands Inn $$-$$$
Grand Anse, International
(☎ 444-4238)

EATING OUT

In the South

Inexpensive	$
Moderate	$$
Expensive	$$$

**Aquarium Beach Club &
Restaurant** $$-$$$
Point Salines, International
(☎ 444-1410)

The Boatyard $$-$$$
Prickly Bay, L'Anse aux Epines,
West Indian/International
(☎ 444-4662)

Bolero $$
L'Anse aux Epines, West Indian/
seafood (☎ 444-1250)

Choo Light $-$$
L'Anse aux Epines, Chinese
(☎ 440-2196)

Cicely's $$-$$$
Calabash Hotel, L'Anse aux
Epines, West Indian/International
(☎ 444-4234)

Conch Shell $-$$
Point Salines, West Indian/seafood
(☎ 444-4178)

**Dr Groom's Cafe &
Restaurant** $-$$
Close to Point Salines International
Airport, Italian/West Indian
(☎ 444-1979)

Fox Inn Restaurant $$-$$$
Point Salines, West Indian/
International (☎ 444-4123)

**Horse Shoe Beach
Restaurant** $-$$
L'Anse aux Epines, West Indian/
International (☎ 444-4410)

Indigo's $$
True Blue Inn, True Blue,
Caribbean/International/seafood
(☎ 444-2000)

International Restaurant $$-$$$
Rex Grenadian, Point Salines,
Continental (☎ 444-3333).
Reservations necessary.

Marielle's $$
Mall 21 at True Blue, West Indian
(☎ 444-4641)

Red Crab $$-$$$
Near the Calabash Hotel, L'Anse
aux Epines, West Indian/
International (☎ 444-4424)

Secret Harbour $$-$$
Secret Harbour Hotel, L'Anse aux
Epines, West Indian/International
(☎ 444-4439)

Villamar Restaurant $-$$
L'Anse aux Epines, West Indian
(☎ 444-4847)

THE EAST COAST

The **parish of St. Andrew**, with a
population of around 23,000, has
the longest coastline of all the
parishes and a rich agricultural
interior with many large estates. It
is the largest producer of the
island's main export crops of
cocoa, nutmeg and bananas, as
well as other spices, fruits and
vegetables, cocounts and
flowers, and also boasts the
Fleary's Teak Plantation and the
Claboney Sulphur hot springs.

There are many roads off the

main highway which lead down to secluded bays and coves, such as Galby Bay, La Tante Bay and Menere Bay with their fine beaches, Great Bacolet Bay and the sweeping St. Andrews Bay. Often the last leg of the journey has to be done on foot, but there are usually well-worn paths to follow. La Tante beach is a short walk from the village, Menere beach is close to Mabot Village, and Babounot beach can be reached from the Hope Estate.

In St. Andrews Bay you can see Marquis Island. The village of **Marquis** lies on the coast just before you reach Grenville. The French renamed the parish Grand Marquis, and the village itself is a small fishing community, although it is also noted for its goods woven from pandanus grass. The tough grass is plaited into hats, bags and mats which are sold across the island, to locals and visitors alike.

The Marquis River runs to the bay from an area of hills known as Mount Carmel where there are two waterfalls. The upper falls, the tallest in Grenada, are a 15 minute walk from the main road. They are known as the **Marquis Falls**, but are also referred to as the **Royal Mount Carmel**

Waterfalls. It is a delightful walk in through the trees, and access has been made easier with the provision of path and signs. Picnic areas and a visitor centre are planned, and there are already vendor's stalls and trail guides if needed.

The lower falls are a little further away and the walk to them along the river is more difficult. These falls are not as high but are much wider. Work on improving access and facilities at both is under way.

Remains of eighteenth century fortifications can be seen at **Post Royal**, scene of a battle during the rebellion, and there are also the remnants of fortifications on top of **Pilot Hill**, just inland and to the south of Grenville, and **Battle Hill**, both overlooking the main town of Grenville, affectionately called Rainbow City by the locals.

Although **Grenville** sits on a wide bay, there are a number of reefs just offshore which have prevented it from developing into a busier port. As it is, much of the produce grown locally is taken by road to St. George's for shipping. The French called the town La Baye, and this term is still used to describe the area in

Facing page: The north-west of the island has several small villages

THE FEDON REBELLION

Under the Treaty of Versailles of 1783, Grenada was ceded to Britain from France. The French settlers who stayed on the island were treated very badly by the British, and on 3 March 1795 they rebelled. They were supported by slaves and the French Revolutionaries in Martinique, and led by Julien Fedon, a Grenadian of Afro-French descent who owned the Belvidere Estate. The 2 year rebellion saw huge loss of life and destruction. Grenville was destroyed and eventually the whole island, apart from St. George's was under the control of the rebels. The rebels were regarded as freedom-fighters by slaves throughout the Caribbean, and the French continued their support in the hope that control of Grenada could be wrested from the British. The rebels made their headquarters in the mountains, and resisted all attempts to unseat them for 14 months. Eventually a huge force of British troops was sent to the island and succeeded in defeating the rebels. Many of the rebels were killed in the fighting, but those that survived were transported back to St. George's and publicly hanged in the Market Square. Mysteriously Fedon himself was not captured and he disappeared without trace.

and around Grenville. The town used to be sited a little south of its present location but was destroyed during the Fedon Rebellion of 1795 to 1796, the first town to be attacked during the island uprising.

The town was rebuilt on its present site, and many interesting old buildings can be seen, such as the Anglican church, police station, post house and court house.

The market is behind the court house and on Saturdays it is packed with produce. Fresh meat, locally slaughtered, is on sale together with fish, crabs, fruit and vegetables, and delicious freshly baked bread. There are beautiful displays of flowers for sale and locally woven and plaited goods. The town is known for tasty local dishes.

A fundraising campaign is under way to raise money to renovate the old Catholic church and convert it into a museum, library and art gallery.

Grenville also has the island's
※ largest **nutmeg station**, open Monday to Saturday during normal working hours, and a visit is a must. There is a small fee for admission and a conducted tour, and the knowledgeable guides tell you how the nutmegs are graded, then separated into

nutmeg and mace, dried, and sacked for shipment around the world. The old station offers the most incredible aromas.

Outside the station, there are several stalls and shops offering spices and products made from them, and these make good souvenirs, especially when packaged together in a hand woven basket made on the island. Benjamin's Variety is a shop/gallery which offers local arts and crafts for sale.

The Grenville Carnival is held during the second week of August, and includes the 'Rainbow City Festival of Arts', which features local arts, crafts and entertainments, sporting events, competitions and concerts. During the first weekend of the month, the market is filled with booths displaying local arts and crafts, as well as culinary skills such as jams and preserves and sweets.

Just north of town is **Pearls**, site of Grenada's first airport. It was in use from 1943 until the Point Salines International Airport opened in 1984. The runway is still littered with debris scattered over it to prevent take-offs and landings at the time of the US invasion. Two planes, one Russian and the other Cuban, still lie at the end of the runway.

The district has now been declared an archaeological site of international importance because it was the site of one of the largest Arawak Amerindian settlements in the Caribbean. It is illegal to dig or remove any artifacts from the area. Just inland from the airport is the old Dunfermline Sugar Factory, now a rum distillery.

The area around Pearls is also known for its beaches, but the seas can be rough and there are often strong currents and undertows, and just before you reach town there is an old windmill close to the road, although it has lost its sails.

At **Carlton Junction**, open Monday to Saturday during the day, you can see how cocoa is processed. The Cocoa Fermentary buys cocoa from the farmers and then gets it ready for export. There are government agricultural research stations at **Boulogne** and **Mirabeau** and both are open to the public

and sell a wide range of plants and flowers. Boulogne is mainly a cocoa propogating station and plant nursery, and Mirabeau researches economic plants and vegetable pest control.

EATING OUT

On the East Coast

Inexpensive	$
Moderate	$$
Expensive	$$$

Bain's $-$$
Grenville, West Indian/ International/seafood (☎ 442-7337)

Ebony $-$$
Victoria Street, Grenville, West Indian (☎ 442-7311)

Sam's Inn $$
Grenville, Grenadian specialities (☎ 442-7853)

THE NORTH COAST

The northern tip of the island is in the **parish of St. Patrick**, which has a population of around 10,000. There are many old estates with fine homes, while others have been carefully

Following pages: Morne Fendue, set in flower filled gardens

restored. The parish is mostly agricultural, supplying cocoa, bananas and spices, as well as citrus and 'ground provisions' such as yam, tannia and sweet potatoes.

The tour follows the main road to Tivoli and then you turn right for the coast and the **River Antoine Rum Distillery**, although today it is part of Antoine Bay, the oldest in the Caribbean. It is open daily for visits and tastings. The 500 acre (200 hectare) **Antoine Estate** with 1½ miles (2km) of coastline, was bought by its French owner in 1785 for the equivalent of £200 sterling. It includes what the locals still call Conception Beach although it is today part of Antoine Bay, which is said to be the first strip of Grenada coastline spotted by Columbus. The estate has now been bought by a consortium of Grenadian businessmen, and is being restored. The rum distillery cannot keep pace with demand for its product, which claims to be the strongest rum made on the island.

The road then continues north running alongside Antoine Bay, with Lake Antoine inland. Three miles (5km) of man-made canals were constructed to carry water from the lake to the water wheel used to crush the sugar cane at the Antoine distillery.

The water is held in a reservoir overnight to build up the pressure and when released, drives a 125-year-old 30ft (9m) diameter water wheel built by Geo Fletcher & Co at the Masson Works in Derby, England. The water wheel is still in operation today and spare parts, when needed, are still available from the manufacturer. Up to 3,000 gallons (13,500 litres) of juice are handled every day, most from cane produced on the estate, which also grows coconuts, citrus, avocados, bananas and lime. The pulp left after crushing is then used to fire the boilers beneath the copper stills which distill the juice into rum, a system which has not changed since 1785. You can learn how rum is made and taste the end product.

Lake Antoine is the flooded crater of an extinct volcano, and another rewarding bird watching area. Many species nest around the lake.

The road then turns inland for a short distance to the **River Sallee Boiling Springs**. The sulphur springs are believed by the locals to have healing properties, and candles are often lit and placed around the pools.

You can then either cut across country to Sauteurs, via Mount Rose where the remains of an old windmill on a knoll have largely been taken over by vines, or follow the coast round Grenada Bay to Bedford Point on the north-eastern tip of the island. From here you can look out to Sugar Loaf Island, Green Island and Sandy Island which lie in an arc running north-west to south-east just offshore. The road then runs west along the coast past Levera Pond on your left and **Levera Hill** 2,781ft (848m) beyond. **Levera Beach** is a great place for picnics and popular with the locals at weekends and special holidays. Much of the beach area and just inland is now a national park, and almost the whole island comes here to celebrate special holidays such as Independence Day. The information centre has details about the area, and guides can be arranged for the walk to the 'Welcome Stone' which offers superb views of the coast and offshore islands.

About 200 years ago there used to be a jetty into the bay which was used to load produce from local estates onto ships, and a fort was built on **Bedford Point** to protect it. The remains of the fort can still be seen, and there are fabulous views from the headland out to sea.

There is a safe beach at nearby **Bathway**, with huge rock pools, and a reef acts which acts as a buffer and takes the force out of the Atlantic rollers. Close by is the Levera Development, where a number of large modern homes have been built. Also nearby is a small cottage industry producing corn straw dolls. Visitors are welcome.

Sugar Loaf Island, named because of its shape, is also known as **Levera Island** and stands in Levera Bay. All three islands have large bird populations but are privately owned so cannot be visited. If you are interested in birds, however, visit **Levera Pond** where you can spot kingfishers, a wealth of waterfowl and many other species.

The main town is **Sauteurs** which gets its name from an heroic incident in the seventeenth century. The French occupied the island but were still fighting the Caribs for full control of it. The Caribs were chased by French soldiers until they were cornered on top of the cliffs overlooking what is now Sauteurs Bay. Rather than be captured, about forty

Following pages: Lake Antoine is the flooded crater of an extinct volcano

Caribs leapt over the cliffs to their deaths in the rocky waters 100ft (30m) below. The town that grew in the area became known as Bourg des Sauteurs, the 'Town of the Leapers'.

You can walk up the hill past the St. Patrick's Catholic School, and through the cemetery to the spot where the Caribs jumped to their deaths. If you have a head for heights, you can carefully look over the edge at **Carib's Leap** and see just how far it is down.

Next to the church, which dominates the town, there is a small candle factory, and the wax is melted in open fires outside before being carried inside and poured into the moulds. Although there are no official opening times, visitors are welcome during the day, Monday to Saturday, and there is usually someone on hand to show you around. There is also a small batik plant in the town which is worth a visit. The young women produce very colourful designs for dresses, scarves, cushions, bags and so on.

Sauteurs is an old town and even at the beginning of the twentieth century, the only way to reach the capital was by boat. A jetty used to run out into the bay and from it, produce would be loaded onto ships bound for St. George's.

Main transport around the time was by horse or horse and carriage, and you can still see the tethering rings in the walls of the Anglican church where the animals were tied while their owners worshipped inside. You can also see the steps that were built in various places to help people get into and out of their carriages more easily. Around this time, a wealthy citizen built a drinking fountain and horse trough so that both riders and animals could get a drink. Although not still in use, the fountain is still standing.

Around the third week of March, the town celebrates the Feast of Saint Patrick, and this has now been incorporated into the St. Patrick's Day Fiesta, which actually lasts for 2 weeks. There are displays of arts and crafts, bands, steelbands, and calypso, as well as agricultural stands and lots and lots of food. The fiesta attracts people from all over the island, and it is a great occasion.

Just over 1 mile (2km) south of Sauteur on the Hermitage Road, Amerindian petroglyphs have been found on stones beside the St. Patrick's river in the village of **Mount Rich**. The locals have planted flowers near the entrance which is sign-posted. The carvings are the work of Caribs and show aspects of their daily life. The large Carib stone carries six carvings and smaller stones in the area have markings but these are not so easily discernible. Some people believe that the larger stone may have been an altar. Headpieces, pottery, implements and tools have also been found in the area, and it is clear this was a major site for Amerindians. It is hoped that extensive archaeological surveys and excavations can be mounted.

Two old plantation houses have been opened to the public serving lunches and dinners to tourists, but reservations are essential as they are both very popular. **Morne Fendue** is a wonderful stone house built between 1908 and 1912, and the mortar used was a mixture of molasses and limestone. It is set in fabulous gardens and you can enjoy a great buffet lunch either in the wonderful old dining room, or on the verandah. The meal usually starts with a traditional soup, and then try as many of the offered dishes as possible, especially the pepper pot. The house has been in the same family for many generations, and the present owner Betty Mascoll MBE, born in England in 1912, the year

the house was completed, still oversees the cooking.

Mount Rodney, another old family home, has the island's typical fret-worked eaves, and tremendous views over the surrounding countryside and out to see with the Grenadines as a backdrop. The house was built in the 1870s and was only recently opened after 15 years of painstaking restorations. Thishouse too, is set in wonderful gardens.

There is a huge subterranean volcano about 7 miles (11km) off the north coast, and the waters over the crater are so turbulent, that boats rock when they pass. That is perhaps why the volcano has the local name of 'Kick 'em Jenny'.

EATING OUT

On the North Coast

Inexpensive	$
Moderate	$$
Expensive	$$$

Morne Fendue Plantation House $-$$
West Indian (☎ 442-9330)

Mount Rodney Estate $-$$
Sauteurs, International
(☎ 442-9420)

THE WEST COAST

The **parish of St. Mark** runs down the north-west coast, has a population of about 3,800 most of whom are engaged in fishing or working on the surrounding estates, and is the smallest of Grenada's parishes. It used to be said that the more palms one owned, the richer you were, which is why many of the old estates here have long rows of palm trees on either side of the drive leading to the main house. The main crops grown are cocoa, bananas and nutmeg, plus other species and ground provisions. The parish includes **Mount St. Catherine** which rises to 2,757ft (840m) and is the island's highest point. From its summit all the island's six parishes can be seen, but the climb is steep and only experienced climbers should undertake it with a local guide.

Although all Grenada's volcanoes are now extinct, hot mineral springs can be found in many parts of the island, and you can visit some on the slopes of Mount St. Catherine, above the Tufton Hall Estate. Tufton Hall was the location of an adventure project set up by the Catholic church a number of years ago, aimed at helping young boys become useful members of society. The boys were fed and clothed and taught agricultural skills, and the crops produced were then sold to help finance the project. A forest reserve now covers much of the area occupied by the central hills around Mount St. Catherine.

Victoria is the main 'town' of the area, which the French called Grand Pauvre (great poverty) when they were in occupation. Today, the locals often refer to it as 'sunset city', because the sunsets from the beach are so spectacular. It is really a large fishing village with a number of old buildings and shacks. A joint venture by the Society of Friends of the Blind and the Grenada National Council for the Disabled has

Preceding pages: Sauteurs Bay from Carib's Leap in north Grenada

established a small mop making industry here, and the products are sold throughout the island. The beautiful and comfortable small, 12 room Victoria Hotel is the only one on the north-western coast.

Every year, the parish celebrates St. Mark's Day with a fiesta at the end of April. Local arts and crafts are displayed, and there are competitions for the best preserves, jellies, sweets and pickles, as well as concerts and other events. The annual harvest festival takes place every Whit Monday in Victoria. All the produce grown in the parish is displayed and blessed by the clergy of all the denominations. Around 29 June, St. Mark's celebrates the Fisherman's Birthday, the Feast of St. Peter and St. Paul, as does every other parish on the island as they all have a coastline and fishing communities. The celebrations are spread over a week, so that each parish can stage its own special events and activities. Every year, however, the small village of **Waltham**, about 1 mile (2km) north of Victoria, has the privilege of starting the celebrations, with priests blessing the fishermen, their boats and nets.

EATING OUT

On the West Coast

Inexpensive	$
Moderate	$$
Expensive	$$$

Patnoe Enterprises $
Depradine St. Gouyave, ice cream/fast food
(☎ 444-8415)

Close to Victoria and lying beside the road on the beach there is a huge boulder bearing Carib markings and decorations. Although washed by the sea, the typical Carib adornments can still be plainly seen.

The **parish of St. John**, with a population of around 8,700 is the final one along the west coast before crossing the boundary again into St. George.

From the area's main town, **Gouyave**, you can take the rather bumpy road up into the hills to the **Belvidere Estate**, where almost every plant and crop grown on the island can be seen, including the breadfruit, introduced into the Caribbean by Captain Bligh. The island's first nutmeg were also planted here. The **Dougaldston Estate** in the hills, can also be visited and you

can visit the spice sheds where they are processed and prepared for shipping. The old sheds are surrounded by fruit bearing trees of all descriptions, including loofah trees, and inside, one of the workers will explain how each of the various spices is handled. You can learn all about clove, cocoa, calabash, nutmeg, coffee and cocoa. While these very informed guides do not ask for any payment, it is customary to give them a small tip for their time and trouble.

The British tried to rename Gouyave, Charlotte Town and both names appear on old maps, although the original finally won through. It has a Nutmeg Processing Station and the town is the centre of a major fishing area, especially for yellow fin tuna which can weigh up to 160lb (72kg) and more. It has cold storage facilities and much of the catch is shipped to the United States. Each night the brightly coloured fishing boats are pulled up on to the beach, known as the Lance, which is just north of the town.

You should also visit the ✳ Nutmeg Processing Station in the town where the nutmeg and mace are graded, separated, dried and sacked for shipping. There is a US$1 admission charge and guides, who should be tipped at the end of the tour, are on hand to show you round and explain the various processes. Afterwards, you can enjoy local cooking at one of Gouyave's eateries. Just outside the village you can also visit the small Mabuya Fishermens' Museum. There are no official opening hours but it is usually accessible from Monday to Saturday during the day.

Continue south along the coast road and you come to **Palmiste** where there is a New Life Organisation's Vocational Skills Training Centre. The project is run by four of Grenada's churches and teaches trades and skills to 16-23 year olds. The trainee carpenters and bricklayers have put these skills into practice by helping expand the centre by building more classrooms and furniture. There is a small craft shop which sells items made at the centre.

Behind the centre on the hillside, there is an artificial lake which has been formed by damming the river, and it makes a

Preceding pages: The main road into Gouyave

charming picnic spot with fine views out to sea.

There is then a road which runs inland to **Mount Nesbit** where there is a small batik factory run by Thomas Sylvester. He creates the designs and his team, which he trained himself, produce them on beach wraps, scarves, bags and other products. As all the designs are drawn freehand, each item produced is unique and collectable.

Further south the coast road runs through Grand Roy and Marigot and then there is another inland road which leads to **Concord Falls**. There are actually three falls in the series. The nearest, which can be reached by road, has changing rooms, washrooms and a small bar which serves drinks and light snacks, and you can swim in the pool at the foot of the falls. There are a number of stalls close to the falls selling souvenirs and local arts and crafts. The other two falls in the series are accessible if you are prepared for a 45-minute plus scramble along the river bank, but as the river has now been damned to provide clean drinking water, bathing in the Upper Falls is illegal. The volume of water

flowing over the falls can drop dramatically during the dry season. The third fall is the most spectacular with a 65ft (20m) cascade.

It is common to see the women doing their washing in the clear running streams, and during the dry season, the people often bathe in the streams as well as water is scarce.

From the falls you can also continue inland for the climb up to Fedon's Camp and the volcanic **Mount Qua Qua**, part of the Belvidere Mountain Range. The camp at 2,509ft (765m), is close to St. John's eastern boundary with St. Andrew's, and you can climb the steep hill to where Fedon made his headquarters during the uprising. It is a fairly hard climb, but fit walkers should have no problems making it up the trail. When you reach Fedon's Camp, you are not only rewarded with spectacular views, you can appreciate why it was so difficult to dislodge him from his mountain headquarters, and what a feat it was to haul cannon all the way to the summit. Mount Qua Qua can also be reached by a trail which continues on to the Grand Etang,

Following pages: Upper Concord Falls (left) and Lower Concord Falls (right)

and from the summit at 2,300ft (701m) there are the best views of Crater Lake.

If you return to the coast road you can look and drive down to **Black Bay** which gets its name from its black, fine sand. There is an old water wheel beside the road down to the beach, that was once used to crush the juice out of sugar cane.

If you are careful, you can spot a memorial beside the main road out of Concord. It commemorates a fatal accident on 16 January 1991 when a huge boulder weighing around 60 tons, crashed down on a school bus, killing 8 children and the driver. The boulder was so large that there was no lifting gear on the island capable of moving it, so it had to be blasted apart. The memorial was unveiled by the Prime Minister.

The Fisherman's Birthday is the main event of the parish and takes place on 29 June. The fishermen, their boats and nets are blessed by local clergy, and the rest of the day is spent with boat races and other entertainments. Stalls selling food and drink are set up on the streets, and the celebrations continue well into the night with singing, music and dancing.

The road runs south along the coast through Brizan, and just past Moliniere Point, there is a road which leads to **Mount Moritz**, a couple of miles inland which has an interesting history. The community was founded in the nineteenth century by English workers from Barbados who lost their jobs and became destitute after Emancipation led to the closure of many plantations. These people could not find work and appealed to the Anglican church for help. The church relocated them to Grenada and founded the colony at Mount Moritz.

THE INTERIOR

The best way of exploring the spectacular interior is to drive from St. George's north-east through the **Grand Etang Forest Reserve**, and then get out and walk one of the main hiking trails. Guides are available if you want to get the most out of your visit.

Grand Etang lake was formed

about 12,000 years ago, and is about 1,740ft (530m) above sea level. The lake is surrounded by forest, and the nearby **Grand Etang Forest Centre** has information about the wildlife, forestry and vegetation in the area, as well as information about the region's history and culture. The centre's gardens are well tended and worth a visit in their own right, and keep an eye out for monkeys, hummingbirds and shuffling armadillos which all live in the area. A dam has been built on the lake's outlet stream which has raised the water level by around 5ft (1½m), which will be used to supplement supplies during the four driest months. A pump house raises the water to a point near the forestry house, from where it flows by gravity into a tributary of the Beausejour River where the Annandale Treatment Plant is sited. The **Annandale Waterfalls** are reached by the Beaulieu Valley, and are on the outskirts of Willis, about 15 minutes drive from St. George's.

The Concord Trail allows you to reach Mount Qua Qua, and the summit, if not cloaked in clouds, offers spectacular views, and a detour off the Concord Trail will take you to Fedon's Camp. Other walks from the forest centre include the easy but interesting Morne La Baye trail which although it takes only 15 to 20 minutes, allows you to see a geat deal of the area's flora.

THE GRENADINES

An arbitrary line drawn through the Grenadines as part of the Treaty of Versailles, determines their sovereignty. The islands south of the line gives Grenada administrative responsibility for and sovereignty of Carriacou and Petit Martinique, while those north of the line come under the jurisdiction on St. Vincent. Strangely, the line actually cuts across the northern tips of Carriacou and Petit Martinique, which means that Rapid Point, the most northerly point on Carriacou, is actually in St. Vincent's territory.

Following page: Guides are available for exploring Grenada's rain forest

CARRIACOU

The island, to the north, north-west of Grenada, covers an area of 13sq miles (34sq km), and with a population of around 7,000 is the most populated of the Grenadines. The island is believed to have got its name from the Carib for 'land of reefs', and in the seventeenth and eighteenth centuries was spelt Kayryouacou.

Many of the other islands in the chain are no more than islets or uninhabited rocks. Isle de Rhonde, however, about 8 miles (13km) north-east of Grenada, has a small resident community. The Grenadines are especially popular with yachtsmen because of the year round good sailing weather and safe anchorages.

Carriacou was formed as a result of a volcanic eruption at least 26 million years ago. Two thirds of the island is of volcanic origin and one third fossil-bearing limestone, suggesting that after the eruption, the volcano may have subsided under the sea, only to be raised above it again millions of years later as a result of uplift.

The vegetation is determined by the season and the amount of water available. In times of drought, especially in the first 6 months of the year, dry scrub and

CARRIACOU – ISLAND TRAVEL

Getting There: There is a regular schooner service from Grenada which takes 3½ to 4 hours, and day trips can be arranged to visit some of the offshore islands. Boats leave the Carenage for Carriacou on Tuesday, Wednesday, Friday and Sunday mornings and on Saturday and Sunday evenings, but times vary so check. The fare is EC$20 for a single ticket and EC$30 for a return (EC$35 at weekends). They leave Hillsborough on Monday, Wednesday, Thursday and Saturday mornings and on Sunday at 5pm, but always check sailing times.

There are also daily flights into the island's Lauriston Airport, with its 2,700ft (823m) long airstrip. The flight takes 20 minutes from Grenada.

Getting Around: There are lots of roads and hiking trails. Mini buses run from Hillsborough to Bogles, Windward and Tyrrel Bays. The fare is EC$2 and taxis are also available.

cactus predominate. There are large areas of scrub vegetation such as croton, on the western side of the island, while the eastern beaches are fringed with coconut palms, manchineel and sea grape. There are well established mangrove swamps at Petit Carenage Bay on the north coast, and this area also teems with birdlife.

The most common tree on the island is the gumbo limbo, with its reddish bark. Both the dogwood and white immortelle are found on Carriacou but not Grenada. The dogwoods can be seen beside the road between Beausejour and Craigston, and the white immortelles at Top Hill. Many species of cacti, tamarind, bougainvillea and flamboyant abound, as well as coconut, almonds, sugar apple, limes and papaya.

The French were the first European settlers, and in 1750 when the island's first census was carried out, Carriacou had a population of 199 — 92 whites, 92 'negroes' and 15 'mulattoes', but by 1776 this had rocketed to 86 whites and 3,153 slaves. There were 47 estates on the island, 22 were English or Scottish owned, 21 were French owned, and the remaining 4 were owned by 'free' negroes.

The Scots settled Dumfries on the south-eastern coast, and it was until recently the site of a lime juice factory. The pressing plant was built in the early nineteenth century, and there are hopes that it might be restored for its historical and architectural value, particularly its elaborate brickwork. A land settlement scheme was started in 1903 to encourage more people to move to the island.

Carriacou has more than 80 miles (129km) of reasonable roads, a legacy from the French, who built them so they could quickly move artillery round the island during their frequent hostilities with the British. Most of the fortifications which housed the cannon have disappeared, but Rapid Point on the northern tip of the island, is known locally as Gun Point because of the ordnance that used to be sited there, while the fort overlooking the main town of Hillsborough, has been converted into a waterworks. The cannon that used to be sited there are now displayed on Hospital Hill, from where there are superb views out to sea.

The roads allow exploration of almost all the coastline, while others traverse the island allowing speedy access between beaches on the east and west shores.

A reef runs down much of the eastern shoreline, taking the brunt of the Atlantic breakers, and the sheltered waters between the reef and coast offer excellent anchorage, especially in Watering Bay, Jew Bay and Grand Bay. Tyrell Bay is the most popular anchorage along the western coast.

Windward on Watering Bay has a long boatbuilding tradition and was founded by the descendents of Glaswegian shipwrights who arrived in the nineteenth century. Over the years it has built many sloops, and several of these still ply between Grenada and Carriacou. The skill of the shipbuilders is all the more impressive when you think there were no power tools available, and almost all the work was done using axe, adze and drill and bit.

Most of the islanders, including the Scottish descendants, can trace their lineage back very many generations, and those of African descent can trace their ancestry back to the African tribes which they came from. The 1750 census actually listed the slave's name followed by their African tribe.

Dancing is an important part of the island's way of life, and many of the dances still performed have changed little since they were first danced as part of tribal traditions and rituals in West Africa. As the descendants of the early slaves can still trace their ancestry back to their West African tribes, so the dances can still be identified as belonging to the Ibos, Moko, Hausam Chamba, Banda, Temne, Arradah and so on.

The most important dance is the Kromantin which is a tribal dance from Ghana. Its other name is Chief Beg Pardon Dance, and each tribe has its own Beg Pardon dances, but it is the Kromantin which traditionally starts and ends most celebrations. Beg Pardon dances are performed to encourage the spirits of revered ancestors on to the dance area so that strength can be drawn from them.

Other traditional dances were performed to appease their tribal gods, bring fertility to the fields, aid healing, while dances such as the serpent dance were for driving out evil spirits.

The Big Drum Dance, or African Nation Dance, is a traditional West African dance performed on all special occasions, and it has also been adapted as a tourist entertainment. The drumbeat, singing and dancing at night, helped the slaves overcome the tremendous hardship and suffering faced daily, and still

PUSHING THE BOAT OUT

The island still has a powerful boatbuilding tradition and when a new boat is to be launched, it is a time for great celebration. The proceedings normally start with a religious ceremony, and then grains of rice and rum are scattered around the boat. A Saraca is held and a Big Drum Dance performed, and then the animals are killed for the feast. Traditionally, chickens are killed in the boat's galley to ensure there will always be food on board, a ram goat is killed at the stern to ensure fair winds, and a sheep is killed over the bow to make steering easier. While this is going on, more wine and rum is sprinkled around the vessel. The boat is then blessed by the priest, accompanied by individuals acting as the vessel's 'godparents'. The sloop's flag is then unfurled for the first time, revealing the vessel's name, the posts holding the boat upright on the beach are knocked away, and to the rhythm of drums and the clapping crowd, it is carefully lowered to rest on its side. Using pulleys, rollers and a tractor the boat is then slowly hauled into the sea. As it enters the water, bottles of Champagne are broken against its sides, and the launch ceremony is complete. As the vessel is anchored just offshore, the partying begins in earnest. The food is cooking over the open fires, the rum is flowing and music and dancing continue well into the night.

provides a strong and tangible link with their past, not only as slaves, but more importantly, before that in West Africa. The drum was the symbol of this eternal spirit, which is why the missionaries, plantation owners and colonial officers tried so hard to ban it.

Traditionally drums were carved from wood, but on Carriacou, it was not unusual to improvise using an old rum barrel with a goat skin stretched taut over the mouth. The staves of the barrel had to be planed much thinner to ensure the right sound. You can see a 'lapeau cabrit' (goat skin) drum like this in the Carriacou Museum. The bottom end of the drum was usually open, but some drums had bases

Facing page: Grand Etang Forest Reserve

covered with sheep skin which produced a different sound giving the drummer a greater repertoire. Other drums include the Cot, which rests on the ground and is used to beat out very complicated rhythms and requires a very experienced drummer, and Bula drums which are held between the drummer's knees. The Cot uses the skin of a young ewe goat which produces a higher note. Traditionally there would be three drummers with the Cot in the middle, and with a Bula or side drum on either side. A casette of the drum music makes an unusual and memorable souvenir.

Other dances have been adapted from Old Creole, such as the Bele dances, Bongo and Kalinder, while there are those that have just developed, like the Chiffone, Checcup and Pike, and some that have been copied from European dances such as the Quadrille, which was popular in both England and France in the eighteenth century. Families and friends often gathered in each others homes to dance, and at the end of the Quadrille a bouquet would be thrown in the air. Whoever caught the flowers had to host the next dance get-together.

Carnival is always celebrated in February, immediately before the start of Lent. Originally a 2-day festival, it now runs for at least a week and includes costume parades, a special children's parade, the choosing of the Carnival Queen, as well as picking the Calypso King and a King and Queen of the Bands. It is a time for music, dancing and partying, and even the most dance shy will find it difficult to resist the foot tapping rhythms of the steel bands. The only way to really enjoy Carnival is to join in, but you might well need another holiday afterwards!

Maypole dancing is another old tradition that has survived on Carriacou, and each May Day schoolchildren dance round the pole plaiting the multi-coloured ribbons attached to it.

Hillsborough plays host to a 2 day regatta held annually and starting on Caricom Day, the first Monday of August. Apart from the events for both workboats and yachts, there are lots of other water and land-based sports, street parties, cultural events and lots and lots of calypso. Yachts from around the world attend this event which has been held for more than 28 years.

The Parang Festival is held just before Christmas and is

another occasion for song, music and dance with street stalls offering a wide range of tasty foods and drinks.

It is a strong part of Carriacou's folklore belief, that the spirits of the dead and living are closely linked, and that dreams are a way for the spirits to communicate with the living. As a result there are a number of feasts and rituals which take place following particular dreams. The Plate ritual follows a dream when a dead person asks for food. A plate of rice and chicken is set on the table with a bottle of rum and lighted candle so that the dead spirit can eat. If the dream is received by a rich person, more food, including goat and pork, is set out, and this ritual is known as the Saraca. A 'Maroon' feast is always held when someone dreams of a large gathering, and they normally accompany a large annual event such as the harvest festival. Everyone brings some food and there is always drumming and dancing.

After someone dies, the Tombstone ceremony takes place. It is believed that the spirit is not finally laid to rest until the tombstone is placed on the grave, whether this takes a few days or several years. All the relatives and friends of the dead person are invited to contribute to the tombstone. While the grave is prepared to receive the tombstone, the tombstone itself is placed overnight in the bed of the deceased so that relatives can speak to the dead person through it. The following day, amid much feasting, the tombstone is installed on the grave. This is a time of great celebration because the dead person's spirit is now at rest, and the festival is accompanied by Saraca, singing, dancing and drumming.

Fishing and agriculture have been the island's mainstays, but tourism is now an important and growing income earner.

There are more than a dozen locally-built sloops which fish daily from Carriacou and Petit Martinique although most of the catch is sold to buyers from Martinique.

A Government-built ice plant at Windward provides ice and fish storage facilities for the fishermen.

Tree oysters, which grow on mangroves in the lagoon at Tyrrel

Following pages: Grenadian markets offer a bewildering choice of exotic fruit and vegetables

Bay, and spiny lobsters caught offshore are local delicacies.

The *Carriacou Islander*, is a 35ft (11m) motor powered catamaran, which has a huge observation window in the hull which allows close up viewing of the coral reefs and fish around Carriacou and Petit Martinique. The vessel also has its own long ramp which provides easy access for passengers on the beach, including those in wheelchairs. Saline and White Islands, just south of Carria-cou, are said to have the best reefs, while those near Sandy and Mabouya Islands off the west coast, are also spectacular.

A Tour of the Island

❈ **Hillsborough** is the main town, and Main Street runs parallel with the coast. It has shops, restaurants, banks, post office and a tourist information bureau. Monday is market day although there are some stalls every day. ❋ The small Botanical Gardens has displays of tropical plants, flowers and trees, and the little 🏠 museum in Paterson Street, run by the Carriacou Historical Society, has Amerindian artefacts as well as exhibits tracing the early British and French occupation of the islands. It has also an African section. The museum is housed in

a restored cotton gin mill and is open Monday to Friday 9.30am-4.30pm and from 10am-4pm on Saturday. The airstrip is just to the south-west of the town, and overlooking the town is Hospital Hill with its redundant cannon.

Sandy Island which lies due west of Hillsborough in Hillsborough Bay is famous for its beauty, palm-tree fringed white sandy beaches, clear blue waters and stunning coral reefs. It is a favourite anchorage for yachts, a popular diving site, and is so scenic that it has often featured as a backdrop for television advertisements.

At **L'Esterre**, you can visit the studio of Canute Calliste, the island's most famous artist. He is a prolific painter and has been known to complete sixteen paintings in one day.

South of L'Esterre is **Tyrrel Bay**, a popular anchorage for yachts, and famous for its boatbuilding and craft work, and the oyster beds among the mangrove swamps. You can visit the oyster beds by boat, and the trail back to L'Esterre is spectacular with wonderful views.

The Amerindian Well at **Harvey Vale** is only a few yards inland from the bay, and its mineral waters are reputed to have health giving and therapeutic qualities.

Harvey Vale is noted for its oyster beds and yachts are not permitted to anchor in the bay.

At **La Pointe** on the south-western tip, there are superb views and the ruins of an old French plantation house. The road then runs round the southern coast, passing **Manchineel Bay**.

From here there are good views of White Island and Saline Island in the bay. **White Island** is a marine park because of its virgin reef and shoals of exotic, tropical fish. The white sandy beaches make an ideal picnic spot and the surrounding waters are great for scuba diving and other water sports.

Dumfries on the south-eastern coast of the island, was one of the earliest settlements, and an historical area has been declared which shows 200 years of history, including life on a plantation.

The road up the east coast of the island passes Grand Bay, Jew Bay to Point St. Hilaire. It then runs around Watering Bay passing close to Dover Ruins, site of the first church on the island, and then on to the village of **Windward**, famous for its boat building, started by another Scot. From here you can take the 20 minute boat ride to visit Petit Martinique.

The road curves round the northern tip of the island at **Gun Point**, which is legally within the jurisdiction of St. Vincent. The road back to Hillsborough down the west coast then passes through **Anse La Roche**, the most scenic beach on the island with coral reefs just offshore. The beach, is private and unspoilt at the foot of the famous High North Range. **High North Peak**, at 955ft (291m), is the highest point on the island and is now protected as a national park because of its natural state.

Continue south and you can visit the **Belair National Park** which offers fabulous views over the north of the island and beyond to Petit Martinique. **Belair** also has old French and English ruins and there is an old sugar windmill. During the People's Revolutionary Government the area was used as an army camp. There are also great views from Top Hill 775ft (236m), and then it is a short hop back into Hillsborough.

Other sights include the Anglican Rectory Garden, once a Bousejour Great House, and packed with history and cacti, and the Ningo Well, the first well built on the island.

ISLAND ARTISTRY

Artist Canute Calliste, known affectionately as C.C. was born in L'Esterre on 16 July 1916 and is Carriacou's most famous artist. He started painting at the age of 9 and his 'primitive' style has earned him international acclaim and an exhibition at the Barbados National Museum. He has also won several awards for his contribution to the development of tourism in the field of art and culture. He still paints at his small studio and gallery in L'Esterre, and is also an accomplished shipbuilder, carpenter and musician, having accompanied tours to Britain and the United States as a violinist.

Frankie Francis is another island artist born in L'Esterre. Although he has had no formal training, he exhibits considerable talent and specialises in capturing the real Carriacou, its landscapes, culture and people, on canvas. Although he still only paints in his spare time, his works are on display in Hillsborough museum and the Yellow Poui Art Gallery in St. George's. He is also responsible for the mural at Tanki's Place on L'Esterre Beach.

Accommodation: There are two hotels on the island, the Caribbee Inn at Prospect, and the Silver Beach Resort at Hillsborough. A number of small guest houses as well as villas and apartments can be rented.

There is excellent fish and shellfish on the island and many traditional dishes to enjoy. Rum is, of course, the island drink, especially Jack Iron, distilled to an even higher alcohol level, and it makes a good souvenir.

EATING OUT

On Carriacou

Inexpensive	$
Moderate	$$
Expensive	$$$

Al's Snack Bar $-$$
Tyrrel Bay, West Indian cuisine
(☎ 443-7179)

Facing page: Traditional boat construction on Grand Anse Beach

Ali's Restaurant & Bar $$
L'Esterre Bay, West Indian cuisine
(☎ 443-8406)

Callaloo Restaurant & Bar $$
Main Street, Hillsborough, West
Indian/seafood (☎ 443-8004)

Kayak $-$$
Hillsborough, West Indian/Creole
(☎ 443-8446)

The Pepperpot $$
Caribbee Inn at Prospect, West
Indian/Creole (☎ 443-7380)

Poivre et Sel $-$$$
Tyrrel Bay, French (☎ 443-8390)

Roof Garden $$
Hillsborough, West Indian
(☎ 443-7204)

Scraper's $$
Tyrrel Bay, seafood (☎ 443-7403)

Silver Beach Resort $$-$$$
West Indian/Continental
(☎ 443-7337)

Talk of the Town $$-$$$
Main Street, Hillsborough, West
Indian (☎ 443-7118). Reservations
necessary.

**What's the Scoop/Gramma's
Bakery** $
Patterson and Main Streets,
Hillsborough, ice cream parlour and
bakery (☎ 443-7256).

PETIT MARTINIQUE

Getting There: The island
can be reached by boat
from Hillsborough. The
crossing takes about 20
minutes.

About 900 people live on the
island which covers 486 acres,
(194 hectares) and is 3 miles
(5km) east of
the northern half of Carriacou. The
island is really one large hill
with slopes running down to the
coast. The eastern shore is
rocky but there are some fine
beaches on the western, leeward
side. Like Carriacou, Petit
Martinique was first settled by the
French and many islanders have
names of French origin.

The island also has a very
colourful history and long sea going
tradition. In the past fishermen sold
their catches in the freeport of St
Marten and used the money to buy
duty free goods which they
brought home. It was not really
smuggling as there were no
customs officers based on the
island to pay any duty to! Fishing, a
little smuggling, and boatbuilding
are still the main occupations. Some
corn and peas are grown and goats
and sheep graze freely over the
hills. Everything else has to
be imported.

Although the island has electricity and telephones, the lack of rivers has made water a valuable resource, and all homes have a storage tank to collect rainwater running off the roof. Many of the island's roads are paved, although they mostly run along the western side of the island. There is a small medical centre, visited by a government doctor from Carriacou once a week, post office, school and a small Catholic Church. Other denominations usually hold outdoor services.

Cricket is hugely popular and the women's team regularly play against teams from the other Grenadine islands. Rounders is also widely played.

The island has its own Carnival, which is held the 2 days before Lent, and at Easter a 2 day regatta is hosted, which includes donkey races and the famous greasy pole competition. The liberally greased pole is suspended over the sea and the aim is to reach the prize hanging at the end. Most competitors, of course, fail and fall into the sea, but it is a great spectacle.

Traveller's Tips

St George's Anglican Church

ARRIVAL, ENTRY REQUIREMENTS & CUSTOMS

An immigration form has to be filled in and presented on arrival. The form requires you to say where you will be staying on the island, and if you plan to move around. Put down the first hotel you will be staying at. The immigration form is in two parts, one of which is stamped and returned to you in your passport. You must retain this until departure when the slip is retrieved as you check in at the airport.

Passports are not required from British, US and Canadian citizens providing they have two documents proving citizenship, one of which must bear a photograph. Visas are not required by Commonwealth citizens, French and German citizens. There is a departure tax of EC$35.

You may also be asked to show that you have a return ticket before being admitted. Visitors from the United States and Canada staying less than 6 months can use their I.D. card to enter, but must have valid return tickets.

If travelling on business, a letter confirming this may prove helpful in speeding your way through customs, especially if travelling with samples.

Having cleared immigration, you will have to go through customs, and it is quite usual to have to open your luggage for inspection. If you have expensive cameras, jewellery etc it is a good idea to travel with a photocopy of the receipt. The duty free allowance entering Grenada is 200 cigarettes or 250 grams of tobacco or 50 cigars, and 1 litre of spirit or wine.

ACCOMMODATION

Grenada has a wide range of accommodation to suit all tastes and pockets, from the five star all-inclusive resorts to inns, and modest guest houses, self-catering apartments and beach cottages.

If you want to eat out and explore quite a lot, it may pay to stay in a hotel offering part board, or one of the many inns on the island, some of them converted plantation homes, and generally offering excellent value for money.

There are also apartments, holiday villas and beach cottages available for rent offering you the privacy of your own accommodation and the flexibility to eat in or out.

Some terms: MAP stands for Modified American Plan ie breakfast and dinner are included. EP or European Plan means bed only and no meals. CP is Continental Plan which is bed and breakfast, and AP for American Plan, means room and all meals. Prices quoted by hotels are usually the rates for single and double occupancy. Prices, unless clearly stated, do not usually include the 8 per cent value added tax and 10 per cent service charge.

An A-Z of Accommodation
$ inexpensive
$$ moderate
$$$ de-luxe.

ALL INCLUSIVE RESORTS
La Source $$$
Pink Gin Beach
Point Salines
(☎ 444-2556)

A luxury 100 room resort with private beach, water sports, 9 hole golf course and health/ beauty treatments.

HOTELS
Blue Horizons Cottage Hotel $-$$
Grand Anse
(☎ 444-4316)

32 rooms with kitchenettes, TV, private patios, restaurant, bars, pool, jacuzzi, water sports and meeting room.

Calabash Hotel $$$
L'Anse aux Epines
(☎ 444-4334)

30 suites – 8 with private pools and 22 with whirlpools, restaurant, bar, beach, pool, water sports, beach bar, fitness centre and conference facilities.

Camerhogne Park Hotel $
Grand Anse
(☎ 444-4110)

25 rooms. restaurant, bar, island tours.

Cedars Inn $
True Blue
(☎ 444-4641)

20 rooms. Restaurant, bar, pool.

Cinnamon Hill & Beach Club $-$$
More Rouge
(☎ 444-4301)

20 rooms. Spanish-style village with restaurant, bar, pool, beach.

Coyaba Beach Resort $-$$
Grand Anse
(☎ 444-4129)

40 rooms. Two restaurants, bars, water and land sports.

**Flamboyant Hotel
& Cottages** $-$$
Grand Anse
(☎ 444-4247)

39 suites and apartments, Restaurant, bar, pool, free diving gear, conference facilities.

Fox Inn $
Point Salines
(☎ 444-4123)

22 rooms. Restaurant, bar, pool.

Gem Holiday Beach Resort $-$$
Morne Rouge
(☎ 444-4224)

17 rooms. Restaurant, bar, beach.

**Grenada Renaissance
Resort** $$-$$$
Grand Anse
(☎ 444-4371)

186 rooms. Luxury beachfront resort, open-air restaurant, beach bar, cocktail lounge, poolside snack bar, water and land sports.

Hibiscus Hotel $
Grand Anse
(☎ 444-4233)

10 rooms. Restaurant, bar and pool.

Horse Shoe Beach Hotel $-$$
L'Anse aux Epines
(☎ 444-4410)

22 rooms. Restaurant, pool, bar, barbecue.

Hotel Amanda $
St. George's
(☎ 440-2409)

14 rooms. Restaurant and bar.

Mace Hotel $
Grand Anse
(☎ 444-4788)

14 rooms. Restaurant and bar.

Mahogany Run $$$
Morne Rouge
(☎ 444-3171)

51 rooms. Restaurant, piano bar, Grenada's only Olympic size pool, beach club, free scuba gear hire, bicycle hire.

Rex Grenadian $$-$$$
Point Salines
(☎ 444-3333)

212 rooms. Luxury resort with restaurants, bars, pools, terrace café, water sports, floodlit tennis and conference facilities.

Sam's Inn $
Dunfermline, St. Andrew's
(☎ 442-7853)

12 rooms. Meals on request, close to beach.

Secret Harbour $$-$$$
L'Anse aux Epines
(☎ 444-4548)

20 rooms. Restaurant, bar, private beach, tennis, free water sports.

Siesta Hotel $-$$
Grand Anse
(☎ 444-4645)

37 rooms. Restaurant, pool and bar.

Spice Island Inn $$$
Grand Anse
(☎ 444-4258)

56 rooms. Luxury hotel with restaurant, bars, beach, water sports, tennis, fitness centre, entertainment, free bicycles, conference facilities.

Tropicana Inn $-$$
Lagoon Road,
St. George's
(☎ 440-1586)

20 rooms. Restaurant, bar and conference facilities.

True Blue Inn $-$$
True Blue
(☎ 444-2000)

10 rooms. Restaurant, bar, pool, yachting and yachting school, dock, swimming in the bay.

Victoria Hotel $
Victoria
(☎ 444-8104)

10 rooms. Restaurant, bar and beach.

Village Hotel $
Grand Anse
(☎ 444-4097)

12 rooms. Bar, pool and games room.

Villamar Holiday Resort $
L'Anse aux Epines
(☎ 444-4716)

20 suites. Restaurant, bar, pool and conference facilities.

APARTMENTS, VILLAS & COTTAGES

Cannon Ball Apartments $
True Blue
(☎ 444-4384)

14 rooms.

**Coral Cove Cottages
& Apartments** $
Lance aux Epines
(☎ 444-4422)

18 rooms. Beach, pool, tennis.

Fairdale Holiday Apartments $
L'Anse aux Epines
(☎ 444-4579)

14 rooms.

Grand View Inn $
Morne Rouge
(☎ 444-4984)

20 rooms. Tropical garden and pool with waterfall.

Holiday Haven Seaside Cottages $-$$
L'Anse aux Epines
(☎ 440-2606)

12 rooms. Restaurant.

L'Anse Aux Epines Cottages $-$$
'Anse aux Epines
(☎ 444-4565)

11 rooms. Beach and boating.

La Source $
Point Salines
(☎ 444-3777)

On the beach with bar and restaurant.

Maffiken Apartments $
Grand Anse
(☎ 444-4255)

11 rooms.

No Problem Apartments $
True Blue
(☎ 444-4634)

20 rooms. Pool, bar, boutique, mini-mart, free bicycles, conference facilities.

Palm Court Apartments $
Grand Anse
(☎ 444-4453)

6 rooms. Restaurant and bar.

Petit Bacaye $
Petit Bacaye
(☎ 443-2902)

8 rooms.

R.S.R. Apartments $
Lagoon Road
St. George's
(☎ 440-3381)

13 rooms.

Seaside Villa $-$$
Morne Rouge
(☎ 444-4668)

Four cottages.

Solamente Una Vez $-$$
L'Anse aux Epines
(☎ 444-4310)

Beachfront villas. Dining area, beach, moorings.

South Winds Holiday Cottages & Apartments $
Grand Anse
(☎ 444-4310)

19 units. Restaurant.

Springfield Holiday Cottages $
Grand Anse
(☎ 440-2515)

Three bedroom cottage.

Twelve Degrees North $$-$$$
L'Anse aux Epines
(☎ 444-4580)

8 spacious apartments. Each apartment has its own housekeeper who cooks, cleans and launders. No children under 15. Tennis, pool and water sports.

Wave Crest Holiday Apartments
$ Grand Anse
(☎ 444-4116)

16 rooms. Breakfast room.

GUEST HOUSES

Bailey's Inn $
Springs, St. George's
(☎ 440-2912)

14 rooms and 2 apartments, with restaurant serving local specialities, bar and boutique.

City Inn $
Grenville
(☎ 442-7714)

Homestead Guest House $
Gouyave
(☎ 444-8526)

4 rooms. Bar and restaurant.

La Sagesse Nature Centre $
St. David's
(☎ 444-6458)

4 rooms. Restaurant, beach bar, water sports, nature trails.

Lakeside Guest House $
Lagoon Road, St. George's
(☎ 440-2365)

10 rooms.

Madame Jardin Guest House $
Point Salines
(☎ 444-3463)

Mamma's Lodge $
St. George's
(☎ 440-1459)

9 rooms. Restaurant specialises in local cuisine.

Mitchell's Guest House $
Tyrrel Street, St. George's
(☎ 440-2803)

11 rooms.

Morne Fendue Plantation House $
St. Patrick's
(☎ 442-9330)

3 rooms. Restaurant and bar.

Palm Grove $
Grand Anse
(☎ 444-4578)

9 rooms. Restaurant and bar.

Patnoe Guest House $
Gouyave
(☎ 444-8415)

8 rooms.

Rainbow Inn $
Grenville
(☎ 442-7714)

14 rooms. Bar.

Roydon's Guest House $
Grand Anse
(☎ 444-4476)

6 rooms. Restaurant serving local specialities and bar.

Simeon's Inn $
Green Street, St. George's
(☎ 440-2537)

9 rooms.

Skyline Guest House $
Belmont, St. George's
(☎ 444-4461)

6 rooms.

St. Ann's B&B Guest House $
Paddock Street. St. George's
(☎ 440-2717)

12 rooms. Bar, games, dinner on request.

Ursula-Glen Guest House $
Belmont, St. George's
(☎ 444-4298)

3 rooms.

Windward Sands Inn $
Grand Anse
(☎ 444-4238)

3 rooms.

Yacht's View $
Lagoon Road, St. George's
(☎ 440-3607)

4 rooms. Restaurant, bar, island tours, self-drive cars, water sports.

Carriacou

<u>Hotels</u>

Caribbee Inn $-$$
Propsect
(☎ 443-7380)

10 rooms. Restaurant, bar, cycling, hiking, nature trails, snorkelling.

Silver Beach Resort $-$
Beausejour Bay, Hillsborough
(☎ 443-7337)

18 rooms. Restaurant, bar, beach, diving shop, full scuba and water sports facilities.

<u>Villas & Apartments</u>

Alexis Luxury Apartments $
Harvey Vale
(☎ 443-7179)

13 rooms.

Gramma's Flats $
Hillsborough
(☎ 443-7256)

Millie's Guest House & Apartments $
Main Street, Hillsborough
(☎ 443-8207)

1, 2 and 3 bed apartments.

Scraper's Bay View Holiday Apartments $
Tyrell Bay
(☎ 443-7403)

5 rooms.

<u>Guest Houses</u>

Ade's Dream Guest House $
Main Street, Hillsborough
(☎ 443-7733)

7 rooms and 16 apartment suites.

Constant Spring Guest House $-$$
Harvey Vale
(☎ 443-7396)

3 rooms.

Hope's Inn $
L'Esterre
(☎ 443-7457)

6 rooms. Restaurant and bar.

Peace Haven Guest House $
Main Street, Hillsborough
(☎ 443-7475)

6 rooms.

The Sand Guest House $
Hillsborough
(☎ 443-7100)

6 rooms.

Seaside Fountain Guest House $-$$
Harvey Vale
(☎ 443-7425)

2 rooms.

AIRPORT & AIRLINES

Point Salines International Airport ☎ 444-4167

Aereotuy ☎ 444-4732

Airlines of Carriacou
☎ 444-4425/2898

American Airlines ☎ 444-2222

BWIA International ☎ 440-3818
(In the US 1-800-JET-BWIA)

British Airways/LIAT ☎ 440-2796
(On Carriacou ☎ 443-7362)

Caledonian Airways ☎ 440-2796

Carib Express ☎ 1-800-744-3333
from the Windward Islands or
☎ 809-431-9200 from other locations.

Helen Air Grenada
☎ 444-2266/4101

Facing page: One of the many small shops offering an excellent choice of goods

BANKS

Banks are open Monday to Thursday 8am-2pm, and Fridays 8am-12noon or 1pm and 2.30-5pm. Banks are usually closed at weekends and on public holidays.

Barclays Bank has three offices, at Church and Halifax Streets in St. George's (☎ 440-3232), at Grenville in St. Andrew (☎ 442-7220), and in Grand Anse (☎ 444-1184). There is also a branch in Hillsborough, Carriacou (☎ 443-7232).

National Commercial Bank (NCB) has eight offices: Halifax and Hillsborough Streets, St. George (☎ 440-3566), Grenville (☎ 442-7532), Gouyave (☎ 444-8353), St. David (☎ 444-6355), Grand Anse (☎ 444-2627), Hillsborough on Carriacou (☎ 443-7829) and on Petit Martinique. The new head office is at True Blue St. George's.

Grenada Bank of Commerce has two branches, at Cross and Halifax Streets in St. George's (☎ 440-3521) and its head office in Grand Anse (☎ 444-4919).

The **Grenada Co-operative Bank** has three branches: Church Street, St. George's (☎ 440-2111), Victoria Street, Grenville

(☎ 442-7748), and at Main Street, Sauteurs (☎ 442-9247).

Grenada Development Bank has two branches: Halifax Street, St. George's (☎ 440-2382), and at Grenville (☎ 442-6464).

The **Bank of Nova Scotia** has two branches: Halifax Street, St. George's (☎ 440-3274), and Grand Anse Shopping Centre (☎ 444-1917).

BEAUTY SALONS & HAIRDRESSERS

There are several beauty salons in St. George's and one in Grenville.

CAMPING

Camping is not really encouraged, but is allowed in Grand Etang National Park, and in school and church grounds on Carriacou. Camping is not allowed on beaches.

CAR RENTAL

There are 750 miles (1,207km) of road on Grenada, most of them paved, and hire cars or 4 wheel drive vehicles provide the best way of exploring the island. If you plan to go at peak periods, it is best to hire your vehicle in advance through your travel agent. Cars can be hired, however, at airports, hotels or car hire offices on the island.

Hire car rates range from US$300 to 400 a week depending on the type of vehicle and the rental company. Average daily rates are around US$65 and this does not include insurance which costs an additional US$15-20 a day.

A temporary Grenada driving licence is required, and can be obtained on production of your current driving licence on arrival at the airport, the police station or the car hire office. It costs EC$30 (US$11) for a temporary licence.

Rules of the Road

DRIVE ON THE LEFT. The roads are generally good and there is a substantial road improvement programme under way. In rural areas, however, you have to be on the look out for potholes, fallen branches, coconuts in the roads and so on. Do not speed because you never know what may be round the next corner. The Grenadians love of cricket encourages them to play at every opportunity, and the road makes an ideal wicket!

Seat belts are not compulsory but is is advisable to wear them at all times. The speed limit is 40mph (48kph) or slower if signposted, in town, and there is no reason to go very much faster out of town because you will not fully appreciate the scenery.

Drinking and driving is against the law, and there are heavy penalties if convicted, especially if it resulted in an accident.

Avoid clearly marked 'no parking' zones or you might pick up a ticket, but parking generally does not pose a problem except in the centre of St. George's.

If you have an accident or breakdown during the day, call your car hire company so make sure you have the telephone number with you. They will usually send out a mechanic or a replacement vehicle. If you are stuck at night make sure the car is off the road, lock the vehicle and call a taxi to take you back to your hotel. Report the problem to the car hire company or the police as soon as possible.

Hire companies are:

Avis
Paddock and Lagoon Roads, St. George's (☎ 440-3936)

Barba's Rentals, Tyrrel Bay (☎ 443-7454)

Budget Rent-a-Car
Point Salines Airport
(☎ 443-7454) and Melville Street,
St. George's. ☎ 440-2778

Coyaba Car Rental
(☎ 444-4129)

David's Car Rentals
Four locations (☎ 444-3038)

Island Rent-a-Car
Westerhall (☎ 443-5624)

Jerry's Auto Service
Lagoon Road, St. George's
(☎ 440-1730)

Maffiken Car Rentals
Grand Anse (☎ 444-4255)

Maitland's Motor Rentals
Grand Anse (☎ 444-4022)

MCR Car Rentals
Paddock Road, St. George's
(☎ 440-5398)

McIntyre Bros. Car Rentals
True Blue (☎ 444-3944)

Ride Grenada
Grand Anse (☎ 444-1157)

SR Car Rentals
True Blue (☎ 444-3222)

Sunshine Tours and Rentals
Airport Road, Point Salines
(☎ 444-4296)

C. Thomas & Sons
True Blue (☎ 444-4384)

Thrift Rent-a-Car
Grand View Inn, Grand Anse
(☎ 444-4984)

Y&R Car Rentals
L'Anse aux Epines, (☎ 444-4448).

On Carriacou

Martin Bullen
(☎ 443-7204)

John Gabriel
(☎ 443-7454)

CHURCHES

The following denominations
are represented: Roman
Catholic, Anglican, Episcopal,
Presbyterian, Methodist, Scots Kirk,
Seventh Day Adventists, Jehovah's
Witnesses, Islam, Salvation Army,
Church of Christ Scientist, Church of
Christ, Baha'i Faith, Mennonite
Churches and Living Word
World Outreach.

CURRENCY & CREDIT CARDS

The official currency on the island is
the East Caribbean dollar although
US dollars are accepted almost
everywhere. EC$ come in the
following denominations: 5, 10, 20,
50 and 100, with 1c, 2c, 5c, 10c,
25c, 50c and one dollar coins.

The banks offer a fixed, and generally a better rate of exchange than hotels and shops. Travellers cheques, preferably in US dollars, are also accepted in hotels and large stores, and all major credit cards can be used in hotels, large stores and restaurants. The island's American Express representative is Grenada International Travel Services, Church Street, St. George's ☎ 440-2945.

Note: Always make certain that you know what currency you are dealing in when arranging a taxi ride, guide, charter and so on. First establish the currency (either EC$ or US$) and then agree a price. It could save a lot of arguments later on. Always have a few small denomination notes, either US$1 or EC$5 notes for tips.

DEPARTURE TAX

There is a departure tax of EC$35 for all passengers over 13 leaving the island (EC$17.50 for children 6-12).

DISABLED FACILITIES

There are facilities for the disabled at most of the larger resorts, but not much elsewhere.

DRESS CODE

Casual is the keyword but you can be as smart or as cool as you like. Beachwear is fine for the beach and pool areas, but cover up a little for the street. Wear a hat if planning to be out in the sun for a long time. Topless bathing is tolerated on private beaches of resort hotels, but not encouraged on public beaches.

ELECTRICITY

The usual electricity supply is 220 volts, 50 cycles alternating current, and most sockets take UK-style 3 pin plugs. Some hotels, however, also have 110 volt supplies which are suitable for US appliances. Adaptors are generally available at the hotels, or can be purchased if you do not travel with your own.

EMBASSIES & CONSULATES

Grenadian Embassies and Consulates abroad

USA
Embassy of Grenada
1701 New Hampshire Avenue
NW, Washington DC, 20009 USA
☎ 202-265-2561

Canada
High Commission of the Eastern
Caribbean States
112 Kent Street, Suite 1610,
Ottawa, Ontario KIP 5P2, Canada
☎ 613-236-8952

UK
Grenada High Commission
1 Collingham Gardens, Earls Court,
London SW5 0HW, UK
☎ 0171-373-7808

Rest of Europe
Embassy of Grenada to the
European Union
Avenue de Arts 24, Box 2B 1040,
Brussels, Belgium
☎ 011-32-2-230-6265

Embassies and Consulates
represented in Grenada

British High Commission
14 Church Street. St. George's
☎ 440-3536

Embassy of the Republic of China
Archibald Avenue, St. George's
☎ 440-3054

The European Union
Archibald Avenue, St. George's
☎ 440-3561

Honorary Consul of France
7 Lucas Street, St. George's
☎ 440-2547

Consulate of the Cooperative Republic of Guyana
Gore Street, St. George's
☎ 440-2189

Consulate of the Netherlands
Grand Etang Road, St. George's
☎ 440-2031

Swedish Consulate
PO Box 345, St. George's
☎ 440-1832

US Embassy
Point Salines, St. George's
☎ 444-1173.

Venezuelan Embassy
Archibald Avenue, St. George's
☎ 440-1721

EMERGENCY TELEPHONE NUMBERS

For police and Fire ☎ 911

For Coastguard ☎ 399

For Ambulance ☎ 434 in St.
George's, 724 in St. Andrew's,
and 774 on Carriacou.

Hospitals:

General Hospital, St. George's
☎ 440-2051

Princess Alice Hospital, St.
Andrew's ☎ 442-7251

Princess Royal Hospital, Carriacou
☎ 443-7400

ESSENTIAL THINGS TO PACK

Sun tan cream, sunglasses, sun hat, camera (and lots of film), insect repellant, binoculars if interested in wildlife, and small torch in the event of a power failure.

FESTIVALS/PUBLIC HOLIDAYS * & CALENDAR OF EVENTS

(check for time and dates)

January
New Year's Day *
Grenada Sailing Festival, Grenada Yacht Club,
Grenada Triathlon, Grand Anse
Spice Island Billfishing Competition, St. George's

February
7 February* Independence Day Celebrations
Carriacou Carnival
True Blue Indigo Yacht Race, True Blue Inn

March
St. Patrick's Day Fiesta Sauteurs
Carl Schuster Round Grenada Yacht Race
Intercollege Sports Day, Queen's Park

April
Good Friday*
Easter Monday
Easter Dinghy Races
Petit Martinique Regatta, Easter Weekend
Easter Monday*
St. Mark's Day Festival, Victoria

May
Labour Day*parades and fetes
La Source Grand Anse Race, Grand Anse Bay
Whit Monday* sporting events

June
Corpus Christi* religious processions and food planting ceremonies
Volley Ball Club Championships
Outfitter's International Cup
South Coast Yacht Race
Fisherman's Birthday Celebrations, Gouyave

July
Venezuala Independence Day Regatta, St. George's Harbour
Carriacou Regatta

August
Caricom Day * held on the first Monday
Rainbow City Festival, Grenville
Grenada Carnival, held over the second weekend

Following pages: Grenadian carnivals should not be missed

October
Thanksgiving Day*

November
Match Racing off Grand Anse

December
Carriacou Parang Festival
Christmas Day and Boxing Day *
New Year's Eve parties and gala
   dances
Midnight Marathon, New Year's
   Eve, a half marathon, Grenville

FISHING

Fishing is an island pursuit, and
many Grenadians will fish for
hours from harbour walls, from
the beach or river side. Deep sea
and game fishing is mostly for
blue marlin and tuna which can
weight up to 1,000lb (450kgm),
wahoo and white marlin, which
can weigh more than 100lb
(45kgm) and the fighting sailfish.
Snapper, grouper, bonito, dorado
and barracuda can all be kept
close to shore. There are a
number of boats available for
charter or which offer deep sea
fishing. Operators and boats for
charter include: Captain Peter's
Water Taxi Service (☎ 440-1349),
the 32ft (10m) priogue Bezo
(☎ 443-5477), Evans Chartering
Services (☎ 444-4422), the 32ft
(10m) pirogue Havada

(☎ 440-2198), and Tropix
Professional Sport Fishing
(☎ 440-4961).

HEALTH

There are no serious health
problems although visitors should
take precautions against the sun
and mosquitoes, both of which
can ruin your holiday.
Immunisation is not required
unless travelling from an infected
area within six days of arrival.

   All hotels have doctors either
resident or on call. The General
Hospital is in St. George's near
Fort George. The smaller Princess
Alice Hospital is at Mirabeau
in St. Andrew's and there is 24
hour emergency medical,
surgical and pharmaceutical
services available at the Black
Rock Medical Clinic in the Grand
Anse Shopping Centre.

   Emergency dental treatment
can be obtained at the Sun
Smile Dental Care Clinic in
the Le Marquis Complex
at Grand Anse.

   The island has a decompression
chamber available in case of
diving accidents, air ambulance,
24 hour casualty department, and
emergency dental facilities.

   The Princess Royal Hospital
serves Carriacou.

IRRITATING INSECTS

Mosquitoes can be a problem almost anywhere. In your room, burn mosquito coils or use one of the many electrical plug in devices which burn an insect repelling tablet. Mosquitoes are not so much of a problem on or near the beaches because of onshore winds, but they may well bite you as you enjoy an open air evening meal. Use a good insect repellant, particularly if you are planning trips inland such as walking in the rain forests. Lemon grass can be found growing naturally, and a handful of this in your room is also a useful mosquito deterrent.

Sand flies can be a problem on the beach. Despite their tiny size they can give you a nasty bite. Ants abound, so make sure you check the ground carefully before sitting down otherwise you might get bitten, and the bites can itch for days.There are several creams and sprays available to relieve itchiness from bites and Bay Rhum Cologne is also a good remedy when dabbed on the skin.

LANGUAGE

The official language is English, although most people speak a patois that is very difficult to under-stand, although it is fun trying to!

LOST PROPERTY

Report lost property as soon as possible to your hotel or the nearest police station.

MEDIA

There are four island radio stations. Radio Grenada, with two channels, is broadcast by the Grenada Broadcasting Corporation, Spice Capital is privately owned, as is Young Sound FM.

Grenada Television broadcasts on channels 7 and 11, and Lighthouse TV, a privately-owned, non-profit making organisation, broadcasts mostly religious and family programmes. Channel 6 is a non-profit making community station offering mostly cultural programmes. Many hotels also have cable or satellite television.

The island also has six newspapers published either weekly, monthly or bi-monthly.

MUSIC

Music is a way of life and the philosophy is the louder it is played, the better. Cars, mini-van buses and open doorways all seem to blast music out, and once the music starts it goes on for hours.

When the Grenadians party, it often lasts all night.

NIGHTLIFE

Most hotels and resorts offer nightly entertainment from local steel bands and island dance groups, to discos and jazz. Worth investigating are the Boatyard Restaurant and Bar at L'Anse aux Epines, Cicely's at the Calabash Hotel, the Dynamite Disco at the Limes at Grand Anse at weekends, and Island View at Woburn which has Caribbean music on Friday and Saturday evenings. Many hotels also hold beach or beach-side barbecues with steelbands, and these are generally open to non-guests as well. The *Rhum Runners 1* and *11* offer evening cruises, including moonlight cruises with unlimited rum and all-night dancing.

PERSONAL INSURANCE & MEDICAL COVER

Make sure you have adequate personal insurance and medical cover. If you need to call out a doctor or have medical treatment, you will probably have to pay for it at the time, so keep all receipts so that you can reclaim on your insurance.

PHARMACIES

There are pharmacies in Grenville (Beckwith's ☎ 442-7312, and Parris ☎ 442-7330), Grand Anse (Gitten's ☎ 444-4954, and Mitchell's ☎ 444-3845), and St. George's (Gitten's in Halifax Street ☎ 440-2165; Grenada in Hillsborough Street ☎ 440-2345, and the People's Pharmacy, Church and Young Streets ☎ 440-3444).

PHOTOGRAPHY

The intensity of the sun can play havoc with your films, especially if photographing near water or white sand. Compensate for the brightness otherwise your photographs will come out over exposed. The heat can actually damage film so store reels in a box or bag in the hotel fridge if there is one. Also remember to protect your camera if on the beach, as a single grain of sand is all it takes to jam your camera.

It is very easy to get 'click happy' in the Caribbean, but be tactful when taking photographs. Many islanders are shy or simply fed up with being photographed, and others will insist on a small payment. You will have to decide whether the picture is worth it, but if a person declines to have their photograph taken, do not ignore this. Grenadans are a warm and very hospitable race and if you stop and spend some time finding out what they are doing, they will usually then allow you to take a photograph.

POLICE

Police Headquarters is in Fort George ☎ 440-1043

POST OFFICES

The Post Office (☎ 440-2526) is on Lagoon Road on the Carenage near the Customs House, St. George's. Post Office hours are 8.30am-4.30pm Monday to Friday. It stays open over lunch but is closed on Saturday. There are post offices in all parishes. Stamps are on sale in most hotels and many shops.

PUBLIC TOILETS

There are not many public toilets on the island, but bars, restaurants and hotels have private facilities which can usually be used if you ask politely.

RESTAURANTS

There is a remarkably large choice when it comes to eating out on the island. There are the inevitable fast food burger, pizza and fried chicken outlets, beach cafés offering excellent value for the money and elegant upmarket dining rooms, as well as restaurants offering a wide range of ethnic cuisines, from creole and Caribbean cooking to Chinese.

Most accept credit cards and during peak times of the year, reservations are recommended.

The restaurants listed in the itineraries are classified by price ($ inexpensive, $$ moderate, $$$ expensive).

SECURITY

Grenada has a low crime rate but it makes sense like anywhere else, not to walk around wearing expensive jewellery or flashing large sums of money.

Do not carry around your passport, travellers cheques or all your money. Keep them secure in your room or in a hotel safety deposit box. It is also a good idea to have photocopies of the information page of your passport, your air ticket and holiday insurance policy. All will help greatly if the originals are lost.

As with most tourist destinations, you might be pestered by touts trying to sell tours, souvenirs and even drugs, or by young people begging. A firm 'no' or 'not interested', is normally enough to persuade them to leave you alone. Don't be alarmed at the large number of people who walk around with machetes. These are used throughout the island as a gardening implement.

SERVICE CHARGES & TAXES

There is a government tax of 8 per cent on all hotel and restaurant bills, and a service charge of 10 per cent is usually added. Menus and tariffs often include these so check to make sure they have not been added again. In shops, the price on the label is what you pay. When buying in markets and from street vendors, try haggling over the price.

SIGHTSEEING

Sightseeing and island tours by land or sea can be organised through hotels, tour representatives or one of the many specialist tour companies on the island. Companies include:

Arnold's Tours/Arnold's Hikes
☎ 440-0531

Barefoot Holidays ☎ 444-4519

Carib Travel ☎ 444-4519

Funseeker Tours ☎ 444-1342

Fun Tours ☎ 444-3167

Grenada Tours & Travel
☎ 440-2031

Happy Island Tours ☎ 440-9069

Henry's Safari Tours ☎ 444-5313

Jolly Tours ☎ 440-9822

Q & K Spice Sunsation
☎ 444-1656

Raymond's Tour and Taxi Service
☎ 444-1283

Rhum Runner ☎ 440-2198

Spiceland Tours ☎ 440-5180

Starwind Enterprise ☎ 440-3678

Sunshine Cruises ☎ 444-1852

Telfor Walking Tours ☎ 442-6200

SPORT

Cricket: This is the national game and played with such a fervour that it is not surprising that the West Indies are world champions. The game is played at every opportunity and anywhere, and just as fervently by women as the men. You can be driving in the countryside, turn a corner and confront players using the road as a wicket. It is played on the beach using a strip of palm for a bat, and even in the water if the tide is coming in. If the island team or the West Indies is playing, almost all the radios on the island are tuned in for the commentary. Wicket-keeper Junior Murray made history on 2 January 1993 when he became the first Grenadian to represent the West Indies in Test Cricket.

When cricket is not being played, football is the top sport. In Victoria there is a football team called the Courts Hurricane. The team was established in 1958 to pull the community together after Hurricane Janet, and thus its name. The Hurricanes have won the national championship more times than any other team, including eight times consecutively!

The Grenadians enjoy running, and triathlons – swimming ½ mile (1 km), cycling 15½ miles (25km) and then running 3 miles (5km) are popular — and the Grenada Triathlon, held every January, always attracts a large field. There is also 'hashing' a fun mix between a paper chase, cross country run and obstacle course. The advantage is that you can do it at your own pace, although there are those who take it very seriously, and the race almost always ends at a rum shop.

For the visitor, there is a huge range of sporting opportunities from swimming and scuba diving, to horseback riding and hiking, to golf and tennis. There is cycling, sailing, squash and, of course, fishing either from shore or boat. The Atlantic coastline offers stronger swell for windsurfing and surfing but the seas can sometimes be very rough and care is needed, while the Caribbean beaches offer safe swimming. Swimming in slow moving rivers and lakes is not advisable because of the risk of bilharzia, a disease caused by a parasitic water-borne worm.

Most hotels offer a variety of sports and water activities, and there are diving schools where you can learn what it is all about and progress to advanced level if you have the time.

Walking is great fun and there are lots of trails, especially in the mountains but have stout, non-slip footwear and a waterproof. Protect yourself against insects, carry adequate drinking water and keep an eye on the time, because night falls quickly and you do not want to be caught out on the trail after dark. Guides can be arranged to escort you on these walks and make sure you get the most out of your trip.

Cycling: Bikes can be rented from Ride Grenada ☎ 444-1157

Fishing: There is excellent game fishing for tuna, marlin, sail fish and

billfish. Many anglers agree that the waters around Grenada offer some of the best fishing in the Caribbean, especially between November and June when migrating sailfish, white and blue marlin and yellow fin tuna are in the local waters. Fishing trips can be organised through Bezo Charters ☎ 443-5021, Captain Peters ☎ 440-1349, Evans Chartering Services ☎ 444-4422, Sky Ride Water-sports ☎ 444-3333 and Sunshine Cruises ☎ 444-2183.

Fitness Gyms/Health Clubs:

Amada Marga Yoga Centre
Near Tan-teen Playing Field, St. George's, ☎ 440-5880

Body Image
L'Anse aux Epines ☎ 444-3254

Body Shop
Grand Anse ☎ 444-4290

Carriacou Fitness Club
2nd Avenue, Hillsborough
☎ 443-8439

Island Magic Massage Clinic
Grenada Renaissance Hotel
☎ 444-3306

Shamar
Lucia Street, St. George's
☎ 440-6880

Golf: There is a 9 hole course at Belmont, near Grand Anse (☎ 444-4128). The club house is open to visitors and offers drinks and snacks. Clubs an be hired and caddies are available. The Grenada Open Golf Tournament takes places in February. There is also a private 9 hole course at La Source, and a new 18 hole course is being built.

Horseback Riding: The Horseman, St. Paul's, offers a variety of horseback tours with guide ☎ 440-5368

Parasailing: Sky Ride Watersports ☎ 444-3333

Scuba: Most of the diving is based at Grand Anse and many of the best dive sites are within a 30 minute boat ride. The best snorkelling is around Molinere and Dragon Bay, best reached by boat, while the headland of Morne Rouge Bay and the reef off Grand Anse can be reached from the land. Most hotels can arrange scuba courses and qualified instructors are able to take pupils from beginner to advanced level. Equipment can be hired.

There are four main wreck sites that can be visited. The cruise ship *Bianca C* is believed to be the

Facing page: Scuba diving at Wibble Reef, Grenada

largest wreck in the Caribbean, and the top decks are about 90ft (27m) below the surface allowing you to 'swim' in the liner's swimming pool. The other wrecks are the *Buccaneer*, a two masted sloop which sank in the 1970s, which lies in 80ft (24m) of water, the *Three Part* wreck in 40ft (12m), and the *SS Orinoco*, off La Sagesse Point, which went down on 1 November 1900. It is in rough waters, however, and only accessible to experienced divers.

Grand Mal Canyon and Red Buoy are the best wall dives, and there are also wall sites at Happy Hill, Halifax Bay, Flamingo Bay and Black Coral Wall. The main reef sites are Bass Reef, Grand Mal Reef, Spice Island Reef, Molinere Reef, Dragon Bay, Whibles Reef and Channel Reef.

Off Carriacou the best dive sites are around Sandy Island, Sister Rocks, Pago Das Garden, Two Sisters on Ronde Island, Mabouya Island and Saline island.

The following offer diving instruction, diving trips and hire equipment: Aquarium Beach Club (☎ 444-1410), Dive Grenada (☎ 444-1092), Grand Anse Aquatics (☎ 444-4129), Karibik Diving, Silver Beach, Carriacou (☎ 443-7882), Scuba World (☎ 444-3333), Silver Beach Diving, Carriacou (☎ 443-7882), Snagg's Watersports, Carriacou (☎ 443-8293), Sunshine Cruises (☎ 444-1852), Tankils Watersport Paradise Ltd, Carriacou (☎ 443-8406), and World Wide Watersports (☎ 444-1339).

Tennis: Almost all the resorts and many of the hotels have their own tennis courts, often floodlit.

Water Sports: Available at all resorts and most large hotels. Dive Grenada offers wind-surfing and sailing instruction, Grand Anse Aquatics offers windsurfing instruction, and Sail Grenada (☎ 444-2000) has sailing classes to suit all ages. Silver Beach Diving and Snagg's Watersports also offer waterskiing and windsurfing, and Sky Ride (☎ 440-9375) offer parasailing from Grand Anse Beach.

Yachting: The eastern Caribbean offers some of the world's best and safest year round yachting, and you can charter boats and crews for the day or longer, or if you have the experience, take it out yourself. There are scores of safe anchorages in secluded bays with beaches that often cannot be reached by land, and full marina facilities at Mount Hartman Bay on the south coast. Prickly Bay is the main yachting centre with a wide choice of charter boats and the Spice Island Boatyard and Marine Services. The Grenada Yacht Club, founded in

1954, also offers moorings to visiting yachts. The clubhouse was destroyed by Hurricane Janet, and the much larger building on a new site was opened over the Whit weekend in 1960. The clubs hosts a number of regattas and events through the year, including the week long Grenada Sailing Festival which attracts yachts from around the world.

On Carriacou there are many good anchorages, and Tyrrel Bay and Cassada Bay are two of the most popular, while Sandy Island is perhaps the most beautiful. There is also an anchorage and jetty at the Silver Beach Hotel, close to Hillsborough. Anchoring in Harvey Vale is not allowed.

On arrival, yachts should fly the yellow 'Q' flag and anchor at least 656ft (200m) off shore. Customs can also be cleared through Grenada Yacht Services, St. George's, and Spice Island Martina. Customs are open Monday to Friday 8am – 4pm.

TELEPHONES & COMMUNICATIONS

If you wondered where Britain's red telephone boxes went, the answer is that many ended up in Grenada. There are lots of public telephones on the island. They are operated by Grentel, Grenada Telecommunications Ltd, a joint venture company handling local and international calls. USA Direct, telegraph, telex and fax services are available through their offices on the Carenage between 7am-7pm Monday to Friday, 7.30am-1pm on Saturday and 10am-12noon on Sunday. Most hotels will also provide fax services.

Worldwide dialling is available from all public pay and card phones. Phone cards can be purchased at many locations including hotels, shops, airports, marinas and tourist offices. The phone cards can also be used on most of the other English-speaking Windward Islands. Faxes and telex services are available through Grentel and most hotels.

The international dialling code for Grenada is 1 809. From the United States, dialling Grenada is a long distance call, dial 1 809 and the seven digit number. From the UK dial 001 1 809 and then the number. Telephone calls from hotels carry a surcharge, are times by the minute and have a 10 per cent government tax added.

In Grenada dial '0' for the operator and '411' for directory enquiries. To ring the US, Canada and most Caribbean countries dial 9 + 1 + area code + number. To use USA Direct, dial 1-800-USA-ATT1

(1-800-872-2881). To use BT Direct dial 1 800 744 2544 for the UK, mainland Europe and rest of the world, dial 9 + 011 + country code + area code + number.

Major credit cards can be used to make international calls. Dial 1 800 877 8000 and quote your credit card number and the number you want to call.

TIME

Grenada follows Atlantic Standard Time which is 4 hours behind Greenwich Mean Time and 1 hour ahead of Eastern Time in the United States. If it is 12noon in London it is 8am in Grenada, and when it is 12noon in New York, it is 1pm on the island.

While it is important to know the time so that you do not miss your flight, time becomes less important the longer you stay on the island. If you order a taxi it will generally be early or arrive on time, and if you have a business meeting it will start on schedule, for almost everything else be prepared to adopt 'Caribbean time', especially in bars, restaurants and shops. Do not confuse this relaxed attitude with laziness or rudeness, it is just the way things are done in the islands, and the quicker you accept this, the sooner you will start to relax and enjoy yourselves.

TIPPING

Tips are not generally added to bills but it is customary to tip waiters 10 per cent, as well as bell hops in hotels, taxi drivers, guides and others providing a service. Tip taxi drivers around 10 to 12 per cent and bell hops EC$1-2 for each piece of luggage.

TOURIST OFFICES

Tourist Information ☎ 444-4140

Grenada Board of Tourism
PO Box 293, St. George's
☎ 440-2279

Canada
Grenada Board of Tourism, Suite 820, 439 University Avenue, Toronto, Ontario M5G 1Y8
☎ 416-595-1339

Germany
Liebigstrasse 8, 60323 Frankfurt/Main, Germany ☎ 069 726 908

Facing page: Grenada is now a port of call for many cruise companies (above), Grenadian fisherman (below)

UK

Grenada Board of Tourism,
1 Collingham Gardens, London
SW5 0HW ☎ 0171 370-5164

USA

Suite 900D, 820 2nd Avenue,
New York NY 10017
☎ 212-687-9554

TOUR OPERATORS

There are many tour operators on
the island and all offer a number of
trips and excursions, or can tailor
make itineraries to suit you.
Many of the tours sound the same,
so check to see that you are getting
value for money, or getting
something special. For further
information consult your hotel or
the tourist office.

WATER

Drinking water from the tap is
perfectly safe although bottled
mineral and distilled water is
widely available.

WEDDINGS

Grenada is becoming a popular
destination for honeymoon

couples, and lots of other
couples get carried away by the
romance of the island and decide
to marry while on vacation.
If you decide to marry, you must:

- have been resident on the
island for 3 working days before
applying for a marriage licence.

- provide all documents in
English or have translations into
English certified by a notary.

- produce a certificate of non-
marriage from a priest, lawyer or
registrar on official note paper,
attesting that neither party is
married.

- produce final divorce
documents if divorced.

- if under the age of 21,
complete a special form available
from the Prime Minister's Office,
St. George's, and have it signed
by parents/guardian and
notarised.

- produce passport and birth
certificates.

- produce EC$25 worth of
stamps (1 EC$10, and 3 EC$5
stamps) to cover Stamp Duty.

Once all the requirements have
been met, all the documents must
be presented at the Registrar's
Office in the Ministry of Health on
the Carenage St George's. The
marriage licence which costs
EC$10 is available from the
Treasury Office. All documents
and stamps are then sent to the

Cabinet Secretary at the Prime Minister's Office in the Botanical Gardens. Allow at least 2 days for the documents to be processed. After the ceremony, copies of the marriage registration can be obtained for EC$2.

Many hotels offer wedding packages and will make all the arrangements for you. The application must be filed at least 5 working days before the date of the wedding. Most denominations of church weddings can be arranged in advance, and registrars usually charge a fee plus travel costs. Valentine's Day is a very popular day for weddings, and registrars are usually very busy rushing around conducting marriage after marriage.

YACHT CHARTER & PRIVATE MOORINGS

There is a huge range of vessels and crews for charter for sailing, sightseeing, fishing and diving. Companies handling yacht charters include: Arnold's Tours (☎ 440-0531), Astral Travel (☎ 440-5180), Bezo Charters (☎ 443-5477), Carriacou Boat-builders (☎ 443-7542), Club Mariner (☎ 444-4439), Evans Chartering Services (☎ 444-4422), Fun Tours (☎ 444-3167), Moorings' Club Mariner Water-sports Centre (☎ 444-4439), New Trend Tours (☎ 444-1236), Rhum Runner (☎ 440-2198), Seabreeze Yacht Charters (☎ 444-4924), Sun Shine Cruises, Grand Anse (☎ 444-1852), True Blue Inn (☎ 443-5477), Windward Islands Travel & Regattas (☎ 444-4732).

There are marina services at: Anro Agencies, Grand Anse (☎ 440-2044), Grenada Yacht Services, Lagoon Road, St. George's (☎ 440-2508), McIntyre Bros, at True Blue (☎ 440-2044), The Moorings Marina, Secret Harbour (☎ 444-4449), Outfitters International, Lagoon Road, St. George's (☎ 440-7949), Power Tripper in L'Anse aux Epines (☎ 444-4106), and Spice Island Marine Services, Prickly Bay, L'Anse aux Epines (☎ 444-4342).

Index

Caribbean Sunseeker

for sun and fun on your island destination, let our *Caribbean Sunseeker* series be your guide. These books have been carefully researched to bring you the best and most accurate information available. This series will include at least the following titles. Check with your bookseller for availability of new titles.

Antigua & Barbuda

Bahamas

Barbados

Bermuda

Cayman Islands

Cuba

Dominica

Dominican Republic

Dutch Antilles

Florida Keys

Grenada

Jamaica

Puerto Rico

St Lucia

St Vincent &
the Grenadines

Tobago

Trinidad

US Virgin Islands